CW00664786

Silent as the Trees

SILENT *as the* TREES

Devonshire Witchcraft & Popular Magic

———— • 🍂 • ————

Gemma Gary

With photography by Jane Cox

TROY BOOKS

© 2017 Gemma Gary

First printing in paperback
August 2017

ISBN 978-1-909602-26-7

All rights reserved.
No part of this publication may be reproduced, stored within a retrieval system or transmitted in any form or by any means, electronic, mechanical, photocopying, scanning, recording or otherwise, without the prior written permission of the author and the publisher.

Any practices or substances described within this publication are presented as items of interest. The author and the publisher accept no responsibility for any results arising from their enactment or use. Readers are self responsible for their actions.

Published by Troy Books
www.troybooks.co.uk

Troy Books Publishing
BM Box 8003
London WC1N 3XX

Cover design: Gemma Gary

Acknowledgements

With Grateful thanks to:
Jane Cox, Inky, the Museum of Witchcraft & Magic
and Scarborough Museums Trust

Dedicated to the memory of
Michael Howard

Contents

Illustrations and Figures

Photoplates

All photography by Jane Cox unless otherwise stated
between pages 72 - 73

1) *North Bovey Village Green.*

2) *A Village Wise Man (unknown photographer).*

3) *The Toad Witch of North Bovey's steen (unknown photographer).*

4&5) *Mariann Voaden and her collapsed cottage (unknown photographer.*

6) *Martha Whitchalse's cauldron along with an 'egg wand' from Umberleigh and 'spell stone' from Yarcombe, MW.*

7) *The Bideford Witches Memorial.*

8) *Cecil Williamson (unknown photographer).*

9) *Cecil Williamson's home in Witheridge.*

10) *Plymouth witch-bottles, MW.*

11) *Human skull spirit houses, MW.*

12) *Pig skull, horse skull, cow bone and chain protection charms, MW.*

13) *A spirit house from Honiton, MW.*

14) *The Dewerstone.*

15) *Soussons Common Circle.*

16) *Scorhill Circle.*

17) *The Tolmen stone.*

18) *Spinsters Rock.*

19) *The Witches' Rock.*

20) *The Devil's Stone.*

21&22) *Wistman's Wood and Inky demonstrates wishtness.*

23) *Squire Cabell's tomb.*

24) *Granite altar and Snake vertebrae necklace used by Devonshire witches, MW.*

25 & 26) *curative charm stones CC.*

27) *Silver florin coin as used to cure seizures, MW.*

MW = artefact in the Museum of Witchcraft & Magic collection.
CC = artefact in the Clarke Collection of Charms & Amulets, Scarborough Museums Trust.

If the time comes when our freedoms so hardly fought for are taken away, and our Mother Earth increasingly threatened, we may need to work again, as Cecil said, in "the Old Ways, secret, silent as the trees in the forest... the Craft works silently, unseen, unsung...."

Jo O'Cléirigh, quoting Cecil Williamson in The Museum of Witchcraft A Magical History, 2011, p.29

INTRODUCTION

As we drove nearer to the remote Dartmoor village the serpentine narrow roads, rising and falling with the hills, were strewn with leaves and fallen tree branches. Had some sudden storm raged through the place before our arrival? It seems not; for thorny tendrils of bramble reached out into the road as they grew apparently undisturbed by the passage of vehicles. I began to wonder; what kind of village is it that we are visiting? Whose roads remain unused long enough to be cluttered with fallen debris and the unhindered progress of roadside briars?

Our destination on that still spring day was the south-eastern Dartmoor village of North Bovey; the scene of a remarkable incident which was to have a profound influence upon the world of witchcraft.

On arrival, we found a beautiful, 'picture-postcard' village of quaint whitewashed cottages arranged around a central village green; with its stone cross, tall trees, and pretty spring crocuses. It was perhaps the very idyll of an English country village, however almost entirely lacking villagers. We were wandering around for some time before any sign of local human life was made, when an elderly lady came by walking her dog. Perhaps North Bovey, like so many picturesque villages here in the south-west, is made up mainly of holiday cottages; usually only occupied during the summer months?

Specifically, it was the village green we had come to see for it was here, in 1917, that an eight-year-old Cecil

Hugh Williamson first encountered a particularly violent manifestation of the old rural beliefs surrounding witchcraft.

During a school holiday, Cecil was staying at the home of his uncle; the Revd. William Russell. Playing in the garden of the vicarage, he heard a 'rumpus' going on over on the village green. Here he found a large and noisy crowd, gathered around a small group of farm workers who were attacking and stripping naked a frail old woman. Cecil's instinct was to throw himself over the woman to protect her from her aggressors; an action for which he received quite a beating himself. The reason, it was revealed, the men were attacking this old woman was that they believed she was a witch, and that she had placed the 'evil eye' on their cattle. Their aim was to expose her 'witch's nipple' in order to prove her guilt, and to scratch forth blood from her body; an old method for nullifying a witch's power.

It was this incident, revealing to him the strength and survival of the old witch beliefs, which resulted in Cecil Williamson perusing a life-long interest in the strange world of witchcraft and magic. Not only would he go on to become a practitioner himself, he would of course also open what is today the world famous Museum of Witchcraft and Magic, attracting the attention and involvement of Gerald B. Gardner in the museum's formative days on the Isle of Man. It was Gardner, of course, who would be the founder of the neo Pagan witchcraft movement known as Wicca. It was Cecil Williamson who introduced Doreen Valiente to Gardner,[1] resulting in her writing much of the 'Gardnerian' Book of Shadows as well as much of the Wiccan liturgy used today throughout the world.

Rather than creating a new religion however, Cecil Williamson's focus of interest remained with the operative magic of what he called the old 'wayside

---

1. Valiente, Doreen. *The Rebirth of Witchcraft*, p. 15 & 37.

witches', particularly those of his native Devon as well as Cornwall, and the 'spirit forces' they worked with.

Devonshire, like its western neighbour Cornwall, is a landscape historically steeped in witchcraft, occult and folk-magical activity. The traditional occupations of Devon's people; namely mining, farming and seafaring, are each heavily laden with their attendant superstitions, rituals and magical acts. 'Superstitions' and belief in spirits, and the efficacy of rural magic, perhaps thrived in what would, well into the 20th century, have been rather isolated communities; nestled in a landscape of hills, strange stones and fertile fields, and cloaked here and there in the secrecy of woodland's cover. It is a landscape enchanted with a rich folklore of its own; perhaps nurturing amongst its people a tendency towards an awareness of the magical and the otherworldly.

Here though was also an awareness of the possibility of coming to harm, via the agency of spirits and magic of a darker dye. Such fears were nurtured, at least in some way perhaps, by the presence at Devon's midst of the eerie, bleak and treacherous expanse of Dartmoor; a heavily haunted landscape birthing forth its own distinctly dark folklore, and the hunting ground of the Devil himself.

And so, within these pages, it is the witchcraft, folk magic, occult lore, spirits, and the many Devil-haunted stones and landscape features of old Devonshire that I set out to explore. First though, it is Devon's own 'wayside witches' and other magical characters we shall meet, both from folklore and from history. In exploring their stories, we often gain a valuable glimpse into their ways; the witch-charms and magical rites of old Devon.

George Martin.

DEVONSHIRE'S
WITCHES & MAGICIANS

———————— • 🌿 • ————————

rom at least the 16th century, the term 'witch' was broadly applied to all manner of magical practitioners who might otherwise be known as wise women, cunning men, healers, pellars and charmers; all providing their own brand of helpful, operative magic.[2] Of course, there was also the practitioner regarded as entirely malevolent in their activities for whom 'witch' was always their sole title, and so the widely used 'white witch' was a handy blanket term to apply to all other practitioners whose skills were available to conjure and to cure. Such 'helpful witches' would be able to offer a variety of services including the lifting of curses, exorcising troublesome spirits, divining thieves and the location of stolen or lost property, charming away illnesses, providing herbal cures, securing love, and protection from harm and ill-fortune.

In the stories gathered about legendry witches, and the accounts of historical practitioners, we are often given fascinating glimpses into the old magical methods, the rites and charms of Devonshire's witches, as well as the beliefs held about them by the ordinary folk through their interactions with the workers of magic.

Caulks of Exeter 🌿

The city of Exeter, the county town of Devon, has been home to many notable professional magical practitioners,

---

2. Howard, Michael. *West Country Witches*, p. 21.

for again and again in the old accounts of witchcraft in the West Country, one reads of an Exeter 'white witch' being visited or sent for to remedy some calamity or misfortune; most often to detect a 'black witch' and lift their ill-influence, in exchange for a fee of course.

One such magical professional of Exeter was known as Caulks. He appears to have been well regarded as a magician, charm maker, diviner and astrologer, and clients would travel long distances for a consultation. Caulks earned 'many a bright sovereign' lifting the influence of ill-wishing from people and animals, and casting divinations by 'ruling the planets' and reading the cards; mostly for young people wishing to learn who and when they would marry. For those 'overlooked' and afflicted with misfortune, he would teach a prayer to be read over the head of the patient; such as The Lord's Prayer recited backwards.

He also fashioned charms to be worn around the neck, or else hung from a nail on the wall, or placed high inside the chimney. These charms consisted of a sewn bag, one inch square, of linen or silk, and into these Caulks would have enclosed one of a variety of magical items, such as 'the fore-foot of a toad, the head of a snake, the liver of a frog, the tongue of a viper, the front tooth of a dead child, or a piece of rag saturated with dragon's blood.'

To counteract the most serious cases of ill-wishing, Caulks might, 'for an extra fee and a few days' free board and lodgings', travel to the home of the victim, in order undertake the appropriate magical operations and 'personally superintend the cure.' [3]

Charity the Toad Witch 🦋
Near the East Devon village of Axmouth there is said to have lived a witch by the name of charity. A story about Charity reveals her to have been of a special class of

---

3. Hewett, Sarah. *The Peasant Speech of Devon*, Preface ix-x.

witch known as a 'toad witch'; being a witch who works her or his brand of magic via the aid and presence of toads. It is said that the toads with which Charity had developed a working relationship were kept beneath her bed in a large old box.

In one of the windows of her cottage was a broken pane, and it was through this opening that the villagers believed Old Charity would travel forth every night upon her broomstick.

As with all old time witches, Charity was believed to possess the power to curse, and her skills in this dark area were experienced by a man who lived in the cottage next to hers. He had tried to keep pigs, but as soon as any pig was brought into the sty, the poor creature would 'turn somersaults' until exhaustion caused them to expire. Because of Charity's reputation for witchcraft, her neighbour naturally suspected his home to have been bewitched to the extent that he would never be able to keep pigs there, and so, of course, he left to live elsewhere in the village. Perhaps, before leaving, he had words with Charity and angered her; for the man was struck with illness that no doctor could understand or provide any helpful treatment for. His suspicions again turning to Charity, the man made a journey to consult with a white witch who, through his divinations, confirmed that witchcraft was the cause of the man's illness and that Charity was the culprit. The white witch told him that the ill-influence could be lifted, but that it would take nine days to be achieved. By his magic, he would cause Charity to be afflicted with illness, and upon the ninth night of her suffering she would be compelled to travel along the street, crying bitterly as she went, whereupon her ill-influence would be lifted. Upon the ninth night, it was said that Charity was spied leaving her cottage via the keyhole, crying loudly along the street just as the white witch had said. The following day, both the man and Charity had been relieved of their ailments and were quite well again.

Old George 🌺

A Devonshire cunning man, by the name of 'Old George', appears in an 18th century story in which he is consulted to discover the thief of a young farm labourer's missing savings. He was an eccentric and picturesque figure; the traditional ideal of a wizard with a cascade of long grey-white hair about his shoulders, who would search amongst the hedgerows and fields for herbs from which to craft his magical philtres and cures. He was also a scholarly type; possessing many strange books and papers via which he could find the causes of things, make divinations, and 'tell the planets'. Girls would often consult him on matters of love and their future marriage prospects. Never though would he ask payment for his services.

Sam, a young farm worker, made a habit of carefully saving what little sums of money he could in a box. Upon adding to his savings one day, he found that the box did not contain as much money as it should. He was sure he was not mistaken as he kept a regular count of the box's contents. To his dismay, he discovered that small amounts of money were disappearing from the box on a fairly regular basis. Someone on the farm was a thief. Sam confided in his friend Jack, a fellow worker on the farm, and the pair agreed that the most likely suspect was a farm maid named Kitty, as she had access to the box's place of keeping. They decided to approach Kitty and ask her if she knew anything of the money's disappearance. Kitty vehemently denied having any involvement or knowledge of the money's theft, and expressed utter shock that the two boys could even consider such of her. Sam's money however continued to be dipped into by unknown hands, and so the two friends decided that they would consult Old George who lived not far from the farm.

On hearing of Sam's predicament, Old George told the two boys to come to him at a certain hour, when the timings 'would be correct' for him to reveal the thief to them by his arte, and so the two young men left and later returned to Old George's home as instructed. They were invited in and made welcome to sit by the fire. Old George made with his hands mysterious gestures in the air, and muttered under his breath words indiscernible to the two boys. Then, into view, as if forming from mist, appeared before them the very image of Kitty, dancing about the room, holding a pair of scissors. After the image had faded away, the old cunning man revealed that he would be able to compel the thief to confess her crime against Sam that very evening.

Later, as the young workers were sat at the farm's kitchen table for supper, the two boys, knowing now who the culprit was, again asked Kitty about the money, and said that if only she would confess and stop, then no more would the matter be spoken of. In a rage, kitty again strenuously began to deny all knowledge, when suddenly she was knocked to the floor and thrown about violently, as if by some invisible force. In terror she screamed out her full confession and promised no more would she take from Sam's savings. Only then did her mysterious torment suddenly stop.

Old Hannah 🏵

Close beside the ancient Dendles Wood, on the southern edge of Dartmoor, an elderly woman, known as Old Hannah, lived with her son in a small and isolated cottage. She was locally reputed and feared as a powerful and dangerous witch; a reputation strengthened by the mystery of how the old woman and her son managed to sustain themselves as they had no known livelihood, livestock or crops, and were generally shunned by the community. Suspicion naturally arose that they had been living on produce stolen from surrounding farms, and when one farmer lost a few hens he openly accused Old Hanna's son of committing the theft. Not long following these events, further losses were experienced on the farm, when a prized horse and some cattle mysteriously fell dead. When the farmer himself fell ill, he feared that he would be next to die, and all agreed that his misfortune was the result of a curse placed by Old Hanna, in revenge for the accusation made against her son.

Something needed to be done; the curse had to be broken and the community were not willing to continue living in fear, so a group of farmers and neighbours decided to confront the old woman and made their way to her cottage. Of course, fearing her magic, no one could bring themselves to make the first move, or indeed make their presence known, and so the angry but frightened group waited quietly under the cover of the woodland's edge; not knowing quite how to proceed. Eventually, Old Hanna's son emerged from the small cottage door with a fine lurcher which immediately began chasing out and catching rabbits with remarkable efficiency, with each one being thrown over the dog's shoulder and bagged by feared witch's son.

At least the mystery of how the pair managed to feed themselves was now solved, but the already angry farmers were now enraged by the sight of what they regarded as their rabbits being so freely taken, and so they forgot their fear (Old Hannah was nowhere to be seen in any case) and broke their cover to confront the young man. However, both he and the dog fled from the scene and the angry group gave chase.

Into the wood they ran, trying to elude their pursuers, yet as some were on horseback they could not manage to evade them, and eventually came to the confluence of Broadall Lake and the River Yealm. With nowhere to turn, the young man and the lurcher made their way in desperation across the flowing waters over the stones and boulders. The dog however was not able to keep grip on the slippery rocks and fell into the water. Their pursuers stopped in amazement as the dog transformed in an instant into Old Hannah herself; desperately splashing about and scrabbling to climb up onto one of the rocks. In accordance with the old tradition that witches, spells, and spirits cannot cross running water, the attempt to cross the Yealm had undone Old Hannah's magical transformation into a lurcher.

The spell against the farmer seemed also to have been broken, for he soon recovered from illness, whilst Old Hannah withdrew and her son ran away, never to return. Much time passed since the incident and nothing had been seen or heard of Old Hannah, and so all believed she must either have died, or followed after her son. Eventually, some brave souls ventured out to her lonely cottage to find out for themselves, and there they discovered her earthly remains; clutching a bunch of broom (planta genista) in one hand, and the skin of a black cat in the other.

Old Moll 🦌

Like most 'old style' witches, Old Moll, who lived in the small town of Chagford on the north-eastern edge of Dartmoor, was what is known in the West Country as a 'double-ways' witch. This meant that she was possessed of the ability to either cure or curse, to bless or blast, depending on the needs of a paying client. Like Old Hannah, and other accomplished witches, Old Moll was also possessed of the ability to 'skin-turn' or shift her form at will into that of an animal; an arte she is said to have been taught by a witch in Taunton. Old Moll's animal form of choice was that of a hare, and in this form one of her favourite sports was to tease the local hunt by leading them on a long and fruitless chase.

In her younger days, Old Moll had been in a relationship with a young man who she jilted in love. For this he never forgave the witch, and swore that one day he would have revenge against her. Being fully aware of her skin-turning ways, he went to visit a local 'wise-man' to see what could be done. Here, he was advised that the only way to kill a witch-hare was to shoot the magical creature with a bullet of silver. So, upon returning home he set about melting down an old silver watch case in order to make the bullet.

Eventually, the man caught word that an exceptionally large 'pussy' had been spotted in a nearby field, and so off he rushed with his shot gun ready loaded with the silver bullet. Upon reaching the field, he did indeed find an uncannily large hare; the largest hare he had ever seen in his life. He wasted no time in taking aim and firing at the animal, however, as can sometimes happen, the barrel of his gun exploded and his right hand was blown clean off.

Of course, news of the incident rapidly spread and fear and suspicion grew to the point that any misfortune suffered in the locality was the fault of Old Moll and her witchcraft.

Rumour existed that Old Moll was at war with another witch living in Widecombe, and so it was decided that the Widecombe practitioner should be consulted to see if anything could be done to stop Old Moll. A consultation was indeed arranged, and the Widecombe witch was all too happy to dispense wisdom that would help defeat her old enemy. To catch Old Moll in her hare form, the old crone advised, a spayed bitch-hound should be sent after her. The folk of Chagford discreetly went about finding such a hound until a fine lurcher was procured for the task.

Everyone kept a keen eye out for the witch-hare and before long she was spotted in a clover field near Rushford. As soon as the report came in a team set off with the lurcher straight to the clover field; letting the dog lose to begin the pursuit.

Old Moll sped off, fully expecting to out run the lurcher just as she had done with hunting dogs may times before, but this time something was different;

she just could not evade the lurcher which stayed close at her heels at every desperate twist and turn. Onward she dashed towards a thick hedge she knew the hound would not be able to follow her through, but just as she disappeared into it, the hound gave a vicious bite to one of the hare's hind legs.

The hunting party, having seen what happened, spied through the gap in the hedge, but there was no injured hare in sight. It was decided that they should go on back to the town, to Old Moll's cottage, to see if they might discover what had become of her.

When they arrived, only one of the party was brave enough to peep through the small window, and sure enough, on a three legged stool by the fire, he spied Old Moll out of breath and busy dressing a serious wound to her leg.

The event had greatly shaken Old Moll, for now she knew she was neither impervious or beyond reproach for her activities. Never again was the witch-hare seen, and the strange misfortunes amongst the people of Chagford suddenly ceased.

Old Snow 🦋

Rev. Sabine Baring-Gould (1834 – 1924) wrote in his *Devonshire Characters and Strange Events* of a remarkable case of magical healing he was personally aware of, which had been performed by a Tiverton 'white witch' known as 'Old Snow'. He must have possessed a good reputation for the efficacy of his work, for as Baring-Gould explains, Old Snow did 'great business'.

The case in question involves a farmer who had caught a 'severe chill' after a night spent out in a torrential storm, trying to divert a stream which threatened to inundate his house.

As a result, the farmer became 'a wreck', having great difficulty breathing and walking bent 'almost double'. Baring-Gould himself became convinced that the man could not possibly survive, and that he would be dead within a year. He consulted with the most famous and experienced doctors and physicians he could afford, all with no success.

Losing faith in conventional medical practitioners, and in desperation, the farmer decided to visit the white witch. From the day of his consultation the farmer rapidly recovered his health. Baring-Gould writes that he did not know what treatment Old Snow provided, but that the farmer was now 'robust, hearty, and looks as if many years were before him.'

Ann the North Bovey Toad Witch ✺

In volume one of *Devon Notes and Queries*, 1901, there is an intriguing account of a witch living and working in the village of North Bovey. Her name was Ann, and she was of that special class of West Country magical practitioner; a toad witch, because to work her spells and enchantments, for good or ill, she employed the aid of her toads.

Ann had many toads, and she housed them in a large and dark old steen which she kept under her dresser. From the account given about Ann, we know the names of three of her toads; they were Croppy, Rumbo and Krant. It was said that Krant was the largest and most wicked of the witch's toads, and the most feared by the villagers. Indeed Ann found some entertainment in the fear the villagers held for her and her notorious toads, and when a visitor came to her cottage Ann would sometimes delight in testing the bravery of her visitor by daring them to go over to the dresser and touch the dreaded steen.

We know also that Ann would perform the traditional form of divination known as 'the Bible and Key'. In order to decide whether or not she should proceed with a magical operation, she would take out her Bible and insert her door key between its pages so that the key's handle protruded, and would bind the book tightly shut. Then she would take hold of the protruding key and stand the book on its edge; if the Bible remained still Ann knew that there was no use in proceeding at that time. However, if the book did turn, then the operation was sure to succeed, and Ann would take out her trusty toads and begin her work.

The details however of Ann's magical work, her mode of operation and in what manner she employed her toads remains shrouded in mystery, and probable deliberate secrecy on Ann's part. Her favoured location for magical working was North Bovey churchyard, and when Ann had a spell or charm to work, she would make her way there, with her toads, under the cover of midnight's dark.

Of course, no one in the village wold have been brave enough to dare follow Ann into the churchyard at the dead of night to find out what the old witch and her toads were up to.

White Witch Tucker 🦋

James Tuckett of Exeter was a seemingly very successful 19th century cunning man known as 'white witch Tucker'. He was, however, not above employing a little trickery and deception to bolster his client's faith in his psychic and magical abilities. An account is given from the *Letters of Nathan Hogg* in *Devonshire Characters and Strange Events* of a farmer who went to consult with the white witch.

Evidently he had suffered a number of misfortunes on his farm, and these, he believed, were the result of ill-wishing directed towards him, and that the culprit was 'a red-cloaked Nan Tap'. Off the farmer went to see what could be done to defeat the old woman and lift her curse.

> *When into Exeter he had got*
> *To Master Tucker's door he sot;*
> *He rung'd the bell, the message sent,*
> *Pulled off his hat, and in he went,*

And seed a fellow in a room
That seem'd in such a fret and fume.
He said he'd lost a calf and cow,
And com'd in there to know as how,
For Master T., at little cost,
Had often found the things he'd lost...

The farmer then proceeded to open up to the fellow client, in what appears to have been the white witch's 'waiting room', about his own troubles and related his own sad losses and his suspicions about Nan Tap. The man in the 'waiting room' seemed so sympathetic to the farmer's plight, and insisted that as his troubles were far more serious than his own, that he should go in to see the white witch first.

When Tucker was ready to receive his next client, the Farmer went into the consulting room, and to his amazement, before he had time to speak, the white witch set about successfully and accurately divining the reason for his visit.

Of course, the other man in the adjoining room was not a genuine client, but someone the witch employed to coax out of his clients the full details of their troubles or afflictions. Tucker was able to hear the conversations with clarity, because the wall which divided the two rooms had an opening which was concealed by having been merely papered over.

The client thus having been suitably impressed and fully confident, the white witch could then administer his charms and procedures. For the farmer, the charm that Tucker provided was a little bag containing some stones that the farmer was to carry about his person, he was also advised to throw water in the direction of the old woman, saying as he did so *'I do it in the name of Tucker'*. If his problems persisted however, he was then to put a faggot up inside his chimney, set fire to it, and as it burned recite a special prayer which the white witch had taught him.

Vixiana ✺

From a 'white', if somewhat dishonest witch of Devonshire's magical history, we come now to a decidedly 'black' witch of Devonian legend. Of course, 'there's no smoke without fire' as they say, and perhaps contained within myth and legend there are distant memories of real events. Perhaps, also, they convey something about the spirit of the places to which such stories are attached.

Vixen Tor is an eerie and towering mass of granite on Dartmoor. Legend tells that this desolate spot was once inhabited by an evil witch named Vixiana, who dwelt within a cave beneath the tor.

It would seem that her powers as a witch were derived from the Devil, and that to maintain these she was keen to give regular human sacrifice unto her dark master. To do this, Vixiana would climb to the top of the rocky prominence, and there sit and cast her eye intently about the moor, looking out for any travellers.

When a traveller was unfortunate enough to be spotted by Vixiana, she would conjure forth a thick and swirling mist to descend, leaving the traveller confused and unable to find their way. Then, Vixiana would call out to them, as though she were guiding them to safety, however, she was instead drawing them towards a treacherous boggy area where many had lost their lives. Once caught, there was nothing the poor soul could do to escape, and Vixiana would delight in their desperate cries for help as they slowly sunk beneath the deep and sucking bog.

One day, however, the witch spied a potential victim who turned out to be no ordinary moorman, but a cunning man well versed in the magical artes. He had heard tell of the evil witch, and the many lost souls she had lured to their deaths, and so he set out that day intent on putting an end to her wicked ways.

As usual, the diabolical mist was conjured down and surrounded the cunning man, who took out of his pocket a magical ring and placed it upon his finger, whereby he became invisible.

Vixiana began her deceitful calls to safety, hoping as usual to draw the man forward towards the tor and into the bog. However, the cunning man deviated, until he found his way out of the mist, and headed on round to the other side of the tor and began to climb.

When he reached the top, he found the witch desperately straining to hear any sign that her trap had caught its victim. She sat there both infuriated and puzzled as to why she could not yet hear any hopeless cries for help, when the invisible cunning man rushed forward and pushed the evil creature from her perch to fall to her death below.

Travellers could at last pass the tor in safety, however, to this day Vixiana's furious and tormented ghost is said to be heard shrieking and wailing around that foreboding tower of rock.

Old Mariann Voaden 🍂

Rev. Sabine Baring-Gould knew and wrote of his experiences of a remarkable witch named Mariann Voaden.[4] She is described as having been 'a picturesque object' with dark, piercing eyes, and skin the colour of mahogany from dirt. The colour red, worn as a scarf or shawl, comes up again and again as a traditional sign of a witch in West Country lore,[5] and it is interesting therefor that Mariann was noted for wearing a red kerchief about her head or neck, as well as an old petticoat of scarlet.

From Baring-Gould's account, it is very clear that Mariann was very much a white witch, or 'blessing witch', and a 'God-fearing soul', however, she still took full advantage

---

4. Baring-Gould, Sabine. *Devonshire Characters & Strange Events*, p.75-79

5. Howard, Michael. *West Country Witches*, p.52. See also Pennick, Nigel. *Daddy Witch & Old Mother Redcap: Survivals of the Old Craft Under Victorian Christendom.*

of the old fears folk held about all witches; even those who specialised in magic of the helpful and curative variety. She expected to receive gifts of food from local farms and households, and would at times encourage such placating offerings. For example, if she spotted a child passing her old cob and thatch cottage, she would emerge, fix the poor child to the spot with a dark gaze and say *'My dear, I knawed a child jist like you — same age, red rosy cheeks, and curlin' black hair. And that child shrivelled up, shrumped like an apple as is picked in the third quarter of the moon. The cheeks grew white, the hair went out of curl, and she jist died right on end and away.'* Of course, a good gift of food, such as a chicken, or a basket of eggs, would shortly be left outside Mariann's cottage by the child's mother.

She did however at times try, in her own unique way, to show her gratitude for the gifts people brought for her, such as the parish rector's daughter who would occasionally bring her food. Mariann made for her a present out of fine lace, and gave it to the young lady on her next visit. However, as she departed with her gratefully accepted gift, Marian called after her *'Come back, my dear, I want that lace again. If anyone else be so gude as to give me aught, I shall want it to make an acknowledgment of the kindness.'* Indeed, Mariann's piece of fine lace work was often given in thanks for some kindness, and then immediately reclaimed.

Mariann seems also to have cultivated her notoriety further by deliberately allowing her once fine old cottage to fall into an entirely dilapidated state; to the extent that people wondered how an old woman could possibly survive in what remained of it winter after winter.

When the thatch began to wear thin and develop holes that let in the rain, farmers offered her straw for the repairs, which a thatcher would have willingly undertaken for free, but she refused, saying *'God made the sky, and that is the best roof of all.'* To keep her head dry as the rains poured in through her deteriorating roof, Mariann sealed up her chimney by stuffing it with a sack filled with chaff and slept with her head inside her bedroom fireplace.

Eventually, her staircase rotted from its exposure to water and collapsed; leaving Mariann having to climb a precarious makeshift ladder to access her bedroom. When the parish rector, concerned for her safety, tried to make her see the dangers of her living conditions, she said to him *'My dear, there be two angels every night sits on the rungs of the ladder and watches there, that nobody comes nigh me, and they be ready to hold up the timbers that they don't fall on me.'* The ladder however suffered the same fate as the stairs and soon collapsed from rot, forcing Marian to live in one room on the ground floor.

When inevitably the whole roof fell in, it brought down the upstairs floorboards with it, forming a 'lean to' roof under which Marian sheltered against one of the walls in her downstairs room. As the door was now blocked, Marian's only way in and out of what little remained of her cottage was a window through which she climbed.

Finally, as water inundated her tiny living space, Marian slept inside an oak chest with its lid propped up by a brick.

Baring-Gould, on a visit to Old Marian, once took his youngest daughter with him. The witch noticed the girl had 'breakings-out' on her face and said *'Ah, my dear, I see you want my help. You must bring the little maiden to me, she must be fasting, and then I will bless her face, and in two days she will be well.'*

Like many a rural charmer, Mariann possessed the ability to stanch the flow of blood from a wound, or 'blood charming' as it is known, and could perform this act even at a distance from the patient. A man once wounded his leg badly when hay was being cut about eight miles from Mariann's cottage. The blood flowed from his leg 'in streams' and a kerchief was dipped in this and given by the farmer to a man who rode with it on horseback as fast as he could to Old Marian. As soon as she charmed the kerchief the blood in the man's wound ceased to flow.

Marian had a book of charms, which she had promised to Baring-Gould, sadly however he was never to receive it, for the remains of her cottage and her few possessions were destroyed by fire. She had been distracted one day, when the local fox hunt, from whom she always received a gift, stopped on its way past her cottage. Climbing out to see them, she left a small fire burning on her floor which caught and spread from the straw lying thereabout, leaving Old Mariann Voaden nowhere to go but the workhouse.

Whilst it is a tragedy that such a valuable artefact of 19th century rural magic; a Devonshire white witch's book of charms, was lost to us, we are indeed fortunate that the Rev. Sabine Baring-Gould was able to record at least some of Mariann's charms and recipes.

For whooping cough, Mariann would cut the hair from the cross on a donkey's back, which she would enclose within a silken bag to be tied about the afflicted child's neck. When asked about this charm Mariann explained; *'You see, Christ Jesus rode into Jerusalem on an ass, and ever since then asses have the cross on their backs, and the hair of those crosses is holy and cures maladies.'*

To cure fits, Mariann would have the patient swallow wood-lice, which could be pounded if preferred but, Mariann insisted, were more efficacious if swallowed *'au naturel'*.

For Burns or Scalds, recite over the afflicted part:

> *There were three Angels who came from the North,*
> *One bringing Fire, the other brought Frost,*
> *The other he was the Holy Ghost.*
> *In Frost, out Fire! In the Name, etc.*

For a Sprain, recite thrice:
'As Christ was riding over Crolly Bridge, His horse slid and sprained his leg. He alighted and spake the words: Bone to bone, and sinew to sinew! and blessed it and it became well, and so shall (name of patient) become well. In the Name, etc.'

Another Receipt for a Sprain:
2 oz. of oil of turpentine.
2 oz. of swillowes.
2 oz. of oil of earthworms.
2 oz. of nerve. 2 oz. of oil of spideldock [opodeldoc?].
2 oz. of Spanish flies.

For Stanching Blood, recite thrice:
'Jesus was born in Bethlehem, baptized in the river of Jordan. The water was wide and the river was rude against the Holy Child. And He smote it with a rod, and it stood still, and so shall your blood stand still. In the Name, etc.'

Cure for Toothache:
'As our Blessed Lord and Saviour Jesus Christ were walking in the garden of Jerusalem, Jesus said unto Peter, Why weepest thou? Peter answered and said, Lord, I be terrible tormented with the toothache. Jesus said unto Peter, If thou wilt believe in Me and My words abide in thee, thou shall never more fill the pain in thy tooth. Peter cried out with tears. Lord, I believe, help thou my onbelieve.'

Martha Whitchalse 🦋

From the North Devon village of Shirwell comes the story of Martha Witchalse.[6] Her reputation was entirely that of the 'black witch', for hers was the power of the 'evil eye', and all who knew of Martha were greatly fearful of being 'overlooked' or 'ill -wished' by her.

She was quite evilly disposed to all in her community, and

---

6. *Gems in a Granite Setting: Beauties of the Lone Land of Dartmoor*, 1905.

remained a lonely and, as a result, increasingly crotchety old creature. Hers clearly was not the power of wisdom. It is said though that the only warm place in her heart was kept for her beloved son, who she had given birth to when wedded in her younger days. Marriage and family life was not to last long however, for her husband died of smallpox, and her son ran away in his youth after getting himself into trouble for stealing sheep up on the moor.

Although she had seen and heard nothing from him, Old Martha's love for her absent son never diminished all through her days. Her one hope was that she would one day see him again.

As Martha grew older, shrinking, wrinkling and withering into feeble physicality, her temper and spite only grew in intensity, and so she was rather taken aback one day when a stranger, walking into the village, approached her and asked if he might have some water to quench his thirst.

Furious that someone would dare speak to her, let alone ask her aid, she hurled a bucket at the weary traveller, screaming at him to fetch water for himself at the brook. Taking up the bucket, the man quietly continued to the brook to drink away his great thirst. Back he came to return the bucket to Old Martha, who by this time found herself quite speechless that the man would dare approach her a second time, and looked ready to explode with rage. The man drew from his pocket a shining gold coin and said to Martha 'if only you had spoken to me with some civility, I would gladly have given this coin to you for directing me to water, yet as you showed me only rudeness you shall not have it.' With that he turned and walked away from the old crone.

Martha fixed her evil eye upon him, stretched out a bony finger and growled 'your time is near, and before three days are done you will know my power!'

The man laughed and continued on his way to a farm near Post Bridge where he was to lodge. On the third day however, he was seized with terrible pains and his life faded fast. The Farmer, knowing the man would soon be dead, asked him if he had any family, and the man strained to whisper with what little breath he had left 'the only family I had was my mother Martha Witchalse who lived in these parts.' Before the dawn of the following day the man had passed over.

When the news reached Old Martha, the realisation that she had taken the life of her own beloved son by ill-wishing, shook her to her bones with a dread and sorrow so deep that she rapidly pined away. Before long, the old witch of Shirwell was found dead on the cold stone of her hearth.

Mother Shipton 🍃

The legendary prophetess and reputed witch, Ursula Sontheil, or 'Mother Shipton' as she became known, is of course heavily associated with Knaresborough in Yorkshire, the land of her birth, but she came to live for many years near the Devon border.[7]

Her mother, Agatha Sontheil, who was also a reputed witch, is said to have given birth to Ursula in the cave which now bears her more famous name, and which is home to the world famous 'petrifying well'. Mother Shipton was known also as 'the Devil's bastard', for it is said that her father was not a mortal man, but a spirit her mother Agatha had encountered as 'a well-dressed, pleasant spoken young man' whilst walking in nearby woods.[8] He took pity on her for she was deeply sad of her poverty, took her as his lover and gave to her many magical powers, including the ability to cure or kill, to conjure forth storms, tempests, thunder and lightning, to have command over man and beast and to foretell the future.

7. Howard, Michael. *West Country Witches*, p.56.

8. *The Life & Prophecies of Ursula Sonthiel, better known as Mother Shipton.*

A journey through some lonely place, while bearing troubles of some kind, is the classic circumstance via which the witch-to-be first encounters the 'Devil' or initiating spirit from whom she will gain her powers and magical abilities. It is a circumstance to be encountered repeatedly throughout the annals of witchcraft history and lore.[9]

Ursula was born, it is said, in 1488 with various physical deformities including 'big bones, large goggling eyes, a long crooked nose and with crooked misshapen legs.' Such an appearance would doubtlessly have added to her own reputation as a seer and witch.

At the age of 24, Ursula married one Toby Shipton, and in time built a successful life for herself as a widely consulted wise-woman for her powers of foresight; particularly among young women seeking some insight into their future romantic affairs.

Being of such an 'unattractive' appearance, many explained her happy marriage by accusing Mother Shipton of binding her husband by the use of a love potion. The couple left to live in Porlock in Somerset where Mother Shipton was often blamed by the locals for any storms or tragedies at sea. During her time in the West Country, Mother Shipton is said to have placed a curse on the Devon village of Silverton because of some offence its inhabitants had caused her. According to the curse, the people of Silverton will never prosper. She is said also to have predicted the very date and time of her own passing many years before the event. When the time approached, she bid farewell to her friends, retired to her bed and duly died.

Sir Francis Drake 🪶

The Elizabethan sea captain, privateer and navigator, remains of course a figure of global fame, particularly in

---

9. Gary, Gemma. 'The Man in Black', *Hands of Apostasy*, p.174-176.

connection with the 1588 defeat of the Spanish Armada. His connection with Devon is also well known, but less well known is his legendary status as a powerful magician, witch, and leader of Devonshire covens.

In c. 1540, Sir Francis Drake was born in the west Devon town of Tavistock. In 1580 he purchased Buckland Abbey, a seven hundred year old manor house near Yelverton on the south-western edge of Dartmoor. Anyone who was seen to have made great achievements and remarkable feats, in the days when witchcraft was widely believed in, was likely to have their successes put down to magic, and some form of pact with spirits. Such was certainly the case with Drake, who was said to have sold his soul to the Devil in exchange for victory and success, and there are numerous tales and traditions of his magical powers and his working relationship with the spirit world. One such tale concerns his alterations to Buckland Abbey.

During the building work, the workmen would down their tools at the end of the day, only to return in the morning to find the previous day's work undone and interference from the spirit world was suspected. Drake decided to find out for himself what was happening and that he would spy on the culprits. As night fell, he climbed a great old tree overlooking the house, and waited. When midnight came, out of the darkness emerged a horde of marauding demons, gleefully clambering about over the house and dismantling all the stonework put up during the day.

Loudly, Drake called out 'Cock-a-doodle-do!' in the manner of a cockerel, crowing in the dawn. The mischievous spirits suddenly stopped their shenanigans in confusion, and Drake lit up his smoking pipe. As they spotted the glowing light in the tree, the spirits believed the sun was coming up and departed back into the shadows from whence they came. Presumably, they were so embarrassed at having been so easily fooled that they never returned, and the building work continued unhindered.

Traditionally housed in Buckland Abbey, is Drake's legendary drum. Beautifully painted and decorated with ornate stud-work, the drum is popularly said to have accompanied sir Francis Drake on his voyages around the world. As he lay on his deathbed on his final voyage, it is said Drake ordered that his drum be returned to England and kept at Buckland Abbey, his home. Here, the drum should be beaten in times of national threat, and it will call forth his spirit to aid the country.

Indeed, there have been numerous occasions when people have claimed to have heard Drake's drum beating, including during the English Civil War and the outbreak of the Frist World War.

In 1918, a celebratory drum roll was reported to have been heard aboard the HMS Royal Oak following the surrender of the Imperial German Navy. An investigation was carried out with the ship being thoroughly searched twice by officers and again by the captain. As neither a drum nor a drummer could be found, the matter was put down to Drake's legendary drum.

During World War II, much weight was added to the drum's legendary protective influence, particularly over the city of Plymouth which, it was said, would fall if the drum was ever removed from its home at the Abbey. When fire broke out at Buckland Abbey in 1938, the drum was removed to the safety of Buckfast Abbey.

Bombs first fell on Plymouth 1940, and again in 1941 in five raids which reduced much of the city to rubble. In all, 1172 civilians lost their lives in the 'Plymouth Blitz'. Drake's drum was returned to Buckland Abbey, and the city remained safe for the remainder of the war.

Like many reputed witches and magicians, Sir Francis Drake was said to possess a familiar spirit to aid him in his work. The presence and influence of this spirit turns up in the stories surrounding his marriage in

1585 to Elizabeth Sydenham, daughter of Sir George Sydenham the Sheriff of Somerset. Some sources say that Elizabeth's parents we disapproving of the union, due to Drake's reputed involvement in the 'black artes', and that the marriage took place shortly before he departed for a long voyage. After no news had been heard from Drake for a number of years, Elizabeth's parents took the opportunity to persuade her to declare herself a widow.[10] Another account states that Drake's departure for his voyage took place before the wedding. In both versions however, The Sydenhams arranged for their only child to be married instead to a wealthy son of the Wyndham family.

It is said that Drake had left his familiar spirit to keep watch over his beloved while he was away, and that the spirit made him aware of her planned wedding to another man. On the day of the wedding, there was a loud clap of thunder, and a meteorite came crashing through the roof of the church. Some said that this had been a cannonball shot from Drake's ship to halt the wedding. In any case, it was taken as a bad omen against the wedding between Elizabeth Sydenham and the son of the Wyndham family.

The meteorite itself, known as 'Drake's Cannonball' has been housed at Combe Sydenham ever since.

Another popular legend featuring Drake's reputed and remarkable magical abilities concerns the creation of the Plymouth Leat. As Plymouth had suffered problematic water shortages through dry summer months, it is said that Drake took his horse and rode out onto Dartmoor to search for a water source. Upon finding a small spring, he uttered a magical charm over it and it burst forth from the rocks as a flowing stream. Drake galloped off on his steed, commanding the flowing waters has he did so to follow him back to the city. Today, the Plymouth

---

10. Howard, Michael. *West Country Witches*, p.73-74.

Leat has its beginning at Sheepstor on the western side of Dartmoor and ends in a reservoir just outside the city.

There are, of course, a number of traditions of magic and witchery surrounding Sir Francis Drake's defeat of the Spanish Armada. He is said to have presided as 'Man in Black' over a number of covens, and that during the threat of invasion, he and his covens assembled on the cliffs at Devil's Point to the south west of Plymouth. There they performed magical operations to conjure forth a terrible storm to destroy many of the Spanish ships. It is said that to this day that Devil's Point is haunted by Drake and his witches, still convening there in spirit form.

Another, more famous legend, tells of Sir Francis Drake playing a game of bowls on Plymouth Hoe when news was brought to him of the approach of the Spanish fleet. In one version he is said to have casually continued his game to its conclusion which, it has been suggested was a magical spell; with the bowls he was scattering with his drives representing the invading fleet. In another version, he stops his game to order a hatchet and a great log to be brought to the Hoe. He then proceeded to chop the wood into small wedges whilst uttering a magical charm over them as each one was thrown into the sea, and as each one hit the water they transformed into great fire ships; sailing out to burn the Armada.

The folklore surrounding Sir Francis Drake also includes his deep association with the Wild Hunt. Sometimes he is seen as leading the ghostly pack of 'Wisht Hounds', and at others he is the riding companion of the Hunt's more traditional leader; the Devil. In some stories Drake rides in a spectral black coach, drawn by black, headless horses and followed by a great pack of black, otherworldly hounds with eyes burning red in the night. Sometimes his coach horses are seen with their heads, and have eyes blazing like hot coals.

One such story tells of a young maid, desperately running across the moors to escape an evil man on horseback she is being forced by her adoptive family to marry. Upon reaching a remote crossroads, and collapsing there in exhaustion, the ghostly pack of hounds and horse drawn coach approach from the darkness. Stopping at the crossroads, a man steps out of the coach, and the young woman recognises him to be the ghost of Sir Francis Drake.

He enquired of the young woman, why she was out on the moor alone and in a state of desperation and exhaustion, and she told him of her plight. Drake pulled from beneath his cloak a box and a cloth, and gave these to the young woman telling her to continue gently on her way, and not, under any circumstance, to look back.

The maid did as she was instructed, and when her pursuer reached the crossroads, he asked of the dark figure in the coach if he had seen a young maid passing by. Drake asked the man to step into his coach, and as he did, its door shut fast and the coach and hounds disappeared back into the darkness. The man was never to be seen again, and it is said that when morning came, his horse was found at the remote crossroads and had apparently died of fright.

According to research by the Devonshire cunning man Jack Daw, there is said to be a family line of Pellars, descended from the girl who encountered the spirit of Sir Francis Drake on the Moor. Their powers, it is claimed, are derived from the gift of the box and cloth he had given to her on that night.

The Conjuring Parsons & Cunning Clergy 🍂

Just as the perceived boundaries between 'witches' and 'cunning-folk' are decidedly blurred in West Country tradition, so too, surprisingly perhaps for some, were the distinctions between folk-magicians and Christian clergy.

Churches themselves, as homes to rituals of divine communion, union, blessing, exorcism and the passage of the dead, are places of useful power and magic. Its water, made holy by its blessing within church rites, was highly sought after for use within acts of popular magic; most often for the purposes of protection and curative magic. Church holy water was so routinely taken for such unauthorised magical uses, that fonts were fitted with lockable covers from the Middle Ages. The Eucharist and the chrism, also being blessed and holy substances, were similarly of use to magical practitioners, and so these, like the holy water, were also ordered to be kept under lock and key.[11]

The Christian saints had in many ways taken on roles akin to elder gods; being often heavily associated with the land and magical loci such as holy wells. The lives of the saints abound with tales of miraculous acts bonded to certain loci, and they were widely petitioned for aid in various acts of magic and divinatory practices. Saintly relics became most sought after as potent magical objects, and even their statues might be scraped to produce powders for use in magical curatives.

It makes sense then that the men who mediated the power of God and the saints, and who administered the rites of the Church would be seen by some to be magicians themselves. Indeed, there were many clergymen who actively practiced in ways that made them virtually indistinguishable from 'cunning men', and in Devon these were known as the conjuring parsons.

Some practiced as astrologers; a service which, despite the disapproval the Church held for such things, they saw as an extension of their normal duty towards their parishioners. One Devonian example of an 'astrologising parson' was the north Devon clergyman known as Parson Joe. His personal notebook, preserved after his death,

---

11. Rider, Catherine. *Magic and Religion in Medieval England*, p.155

revealed details of the horary calculations he would draw up for the people of his parish.[12]

Those clergymen who possessed a more overt reputation for magic often held extensive libraries of books which were rumoured to contain numerous occult volumes and grimoires. These books of power, and the trouble that could arise if they were pried into by the 'uninitiated', feature in a number of popular stories surrounding the conjuring parsons.

One such story is associated with the Reverend William Cunningham, a 19th century incumbent of Bratton. The story tells that while he was absent from his home, his maid, out of curiosity, summoned the bravery to peruse one of the reverend's occult tomes. Inadvertently it seems she had managed to summon two spirits; for a pair of strange creatures 'like chickens' materialised in the kitchen, and she was forced to confess to the reverend what she had done in order that he would then banish them.

The Reverend Franke Parker, known as 'Old Parson Parker' served the parish of Luffincott in the far west of Devon in the 1830s. Like the Reverend William Cunningham, he too possessed a library of magical books, but also possessed, by some mysterious means, the ability to know when someone was prying into his collection. It is said that whilst delivering a sermon, he suddenly stopped and ran from the church back to the rectory much to the surprise of his flock, for he had sensed that his maid was reading one of his occult books. He rushed into his library just in time to stop her before any magical mishap might have occurred.

Some of the magical powers and inclinations attributed to old Parson Parker would appear to paint him more in the hue of a traditional witch rather than that of your average 'cunning man', for he was said to be possess

---

12. Davies, Owen. *Popular Magic, Cunning-folk in English History*, p.82.

the ability to 'shape shift' into animal form. Indeed, the local policeman is said to have discovered the parson sitting on his chair and barking like a dog. Perhaps more incriminating, and certainly difficult to explain, is the situation another visitor to the rectory found him in; laying in his bed surrounded by the bodies of dead toads. [13]

Shortly before his death, Parker is said to have declared that he would return from the world of spirit in the form of an animal, such as that of a dog, a rat or a white rabbit. When he died aged eighty in 1883, so serious was the concern that he would make his promised bestial reappearances, that his body was interred in a grave dug to a depth of seventeen feet as a preventative measure.

Perhaps one of Devon's most famous conjuring parsons is the Reverend Harris, or Parson Harris of Hennock; a small village on the south-eastern flank of Dartmoor with beautiful views over the Teign Valley. Parson Harris was regarded as a 'wizard', and was consulted by the people of his parish for his skills in conjuring, particularly it seems in order to identify thieves and retrieve stolen property. [14]

In one case at least however, it was psychology rather than conjuring that he employed to identify a thief, yet it was his reputation as a conjuror that secured the efficacy of the exercise. A farmer named Tuckett went to see the parson one day; seeking his aid regarding three geese which had been stolen from his farm. The parson reassured the farmer, telling him that the man who had taken his geese shall soon be 'put to open shame'.

On the following Sunday morning, the parson climbed into his pulpit and proclaimed loudly before the seated congregation; *'I give you all to know that Farmer Tuckett has*

---

13. Howard, Michael. *West Country Witches*, p.78.

14. Baring-Gould, Sabine. *A Book of the West; Being an Introduction to Devon & Cornwall*, p.244.

had three geese stolen. I have consulted my books and drawn my figures, and I have so conjured it that three feathers of thickey geese shall now, this very instant, stick to the nose of the thief!' Of course, the guilty party instinctively raised their hand to their nose and the parson, watching for this very reaction, immediately pointed his finger and boomed out across the church *'there is the man who stole the geese!'*

On another occasion, Farmer Loveys called on Parson Harris for help as his fine gander had been stolen from his farm the previous night. The parson set about consulting his occult tomes before drawing a magic circle in which he uttered a strange incantation. He then walked over to his library window and opened it just as the missing gander was flung through to land at his feet, all plucked, trussed, and on the spit ready for roasting.

Another tale, perhaps a different version of the previous one, tells of the parson being consulted about a missing cockerel, which its owner was sure must have been stolen. Parson Harris told the man not to worry, for not only would he conjure the bird to be returned to him, he would cause the thief to reveal himself as well. When the man returned to his home, he was followed by his neighbour who came running through the door carrying the half roasted bird.

A particularly interesting story concerning the parson hints at a dichotomy between his magical artes and his position as a cleric.

He couldn't help but notice one Saturday that his maid, Polly, was caught in a deep melancholy; sobbing to herself now and then. When Harris asked the girl what was the matter, she explained that she was missing her boyfriend terribly; as he had left for Exeter to enter into service.

Feeling sorry for the girl, and of course not wanting an interminably miserable maid about the house, he promised to conjure the young man back home to her. However, the Sunday rolled by and there was no sign of the return of her lover; leaving the maid completely inconsolable, and much shaken in her faith in her master's powers. She went to bed and sobbed herself to sleep.

As Dawn approached however, she was awoken by someone desperately banging on the door outside; it was her lover John, exhausted and drenched with perspiration. The parson's conjuration had not worked upon him until at nightfall when he removed his coat; for in one of its pockets was his Bible. As soon as he took off his coat, he had been compelled to run all the way from Exeter to the parson's home. The young man's Bible had acted as a protective charm against the parson's 'unholy' spell.

THE GALLOWS' LAST

In 1995, a small article appeared in the Lammas edition of *Pagan Dawn* magazine in which Levannah Morgan introduced the idea of creating and installing a memorial plaque for three women; they had been executed in 1682 for causing illness amongst a number of their neighbours by means of witchcraft.

Temperance Lloyd, Susannah Edwards, and Mary Trembles are the last people known to have been executed in England on charges of witchcraft at the extreme tail end of the 'witch-hunting craze'. A small number of executions are said to have taken place at later dates, but these are either not fully documented, or the source information is of dubious authenticity. Mary Bateman, 'The Yorkshire Witch' was executed in 1809, but her sentence was for the charges of fraud and murder, not witchcraft. The last person known to have been sentenced to death in England on charges of witchcraft was the Widow Common of Coggeshall, Essex in 1699, however she died before the sentence could be carried out.

A follow-up piece to Levannah Morgan's original article appeared in 1996, again in the *Pagan Dawn* Lammas issue, giving the news that Exeter City Council had approved the placing of a memorial plaque on a wall of Exeter Castle, and that a stone mason had been commissioned to craft the memorial in slate.

In August the same year, the plaque was installed and can now be found on a wall of Exeter Castle's ruined gatehouse. It reads:

The Devon Witches
In memory of
Temperance Lloyd, Susannah Edwards, Mary Trembles
of Bideford, died 1682
Alice Molland
died 1685
the last people in England to be executed for witchcraft
tried here & hanged at Heavitree.
In the hope of an end to persecution & intolerance.

As can be seen, an additional name has been included with the three originally suggested in 1995. Alice Molland is believed to have possibly been the last person executed for witchcraft in England, after having been found guilty of bewitching a couple in 1684. It appears Alice Molland was sentenced to death by Chief Baron Montagu, however there is no extant documentation to confirm that the execution itself actually took place.

The sad fate of Temperance Lloyd, Susannah Edwards and Mary Trembles however is fully documented, and the circumstances that led to their deaths began on the 2nd of February 1671.

As William Herbert lay on his deathbed he declared that Temperance Lloyd of Bideford had bewitched him. He requested that after his death, his family should view his body so they could see the marks made upon him by Lloyd's witchcraft. He desired also that his son, also named William, should see to it that Lloyd was apprehended for her crime.

On the 14th of March, Temperance Lloyd was accused of bewitching to death William Herbert. A trial took place at the Exeter assizes on the 5th of April 1671 where evidence against her included that given by Lydia Burman, who claimed that Lloyd had appeared before her in the form of a red pig. Temperance Lloyd was acquitted of the charges.

The following year, Lydia Burman died, and her death was blamed on Temperance Lloyd; presumably suspected as an act of revenge for having given evidence against her at trial. Despite the accusation however, no charges were made against her.

Temperance Lloyd again faced charges of witchcraft in 1679, this time for bewitching Anne Fellow. On the 17th of May that year, the accusation was recorded at the Bideford Sessions, and Lloyd was 'searched', but it seems that no further action was taken.

In the August of 1680, Dorcas Coleman of Bideford began to suffer from what she described as 'prickings' in her body. Coleman was taken to be examined by Dr Beare, however he declared that it was beyond his skill to cure her, for the malady had been caused by bewitchment. The following year, another Bideford woman, Grace Thomas, is afflicted with strange pains in her head and limbs on the 2nd of February, which continued until the 1st of August. Then, in late September, Grace Thomas claimed that as she walked up Bideford High Street she met Temperance Lloyd who fell down to her knees and began weeping, and said *'Mistress Grace, I am glad to see you so strong again.'* Thomas then asked Lloyd why she wept, to which she replied *'I weep for joy to see you so well again.'*

In the night following this strange encounter, Grace Thomas was again taken ill with 'sticking and pricking pains, as though pins and awls had been thrust into her body, from the crown of her head to the soles of her feet.' These pains persisted thereafter and were 'much worse by night than by day'.

Upon Easter Tuesday 1682, a poor and elderly woman of Bideford, named Mary Trembles, went about the town to beg for food but had no success. During her walk she met with her friend Susannah Edwards, and the two of them went to John Barnes's house in the hope that they would be able to beg some meat. John

Barnes however was not at home, and the two women were refused meat, bread, or a little tobacco by Grace Barns and her servant.

By June the 1st of that year, the condition of Grace Thomas had worsened to include her belly swelling to twice its size; causing her to cry out that she would die, before lying as though dead for about two hours.

On the 29th of that month, Anne Wakely, an attendant of Grace Thomas, claimed to have seen 'something in the shape of a magpie' appear at Grace Thomas's chamber window. Upon seeing this, Anne Wakely went to see Temperance Lloyd and asked if she knew of any bird to come and flutter at the window. In reply, it is claimed that Lloyd said it was 'the black man' in the shape of a bird.

The following day, Grace Thomas had a particularly severe attack of pricking pains in her heart and head, shoulders, arms, hands, thighs and legs which felt 'as though the flesh would have been then immediately torn from the bones with a man's fingers and thumbs.'

On the 1st of July 1682, Thomas Eastchurch, brother-in-law of Grace Thomas, and with whom she was lodging, complained to the authorities against Temperance Lloyd, resulting in her arrest and detainment on the charges of 'having used some magical art, sorcery, or witchcraft, upon the body of Grace Thomas' and 'to have had discourse or familiarity with the Devil in the shape of a black man.'

The following day, Elizabeth Eastchurch, the wife of Thomas Eastchurch and sister of Grace Thomas, observed nine small wounds upon Grace's knee, and said that each appeared as though it had been made by a thorn prick. On the same day she demanded of Temperance Lloyd 'whether she had any wax or clay in the form of a picture, whereby she had pricked and tormented the said Grace Thomas.' Temperance Lloyd answered that 'she had no wax nor clay, but confessed that she had only a piece of leather which she had pricked nine times.'

Also on that day, during Temperance Lloyd's captivity in the Bideford lock-up, Thomas Eastchurch claimed to hear Lloyd make numerous confessions. As she was returning home from the bakehouse with a loaf of bread tucked under her arm, about the 30th of September 1681, Lloyd is claimed to have confessed to encountering 'something in the likeness of a black man' in Higher Gunstone Lane, and that he tempted her to go to Thomas Eastchurch's house to torment Grace Thomas. At first she refused; saying that Grace Thomas had done her no harm, but eventually the black man persuaded her, and she accompanied him to Grace Thomas's chamber where they found Anne Wakely rubbing one of her arms and one of her legs. Here the black man persuaded her to pinch Grace Thomas on the knees, arms and shoulders with her fingers, and when she had finished tormenting her, she went down the stairs and back into the street where she saw 'a braget cat', a tabby, going into Thomas Eastchurch's shop. This cat, Temperance believed, was the Devil in disguise.

The 'black man', she is said to have confessed, met with her about the 1st of June and told her to 'make an end' of Grace Thomas that night. She duly 'griped Grace Thomas in her belly, stomach and breast and clipped her to the heart' for about two hours. In order that these attacks could be carried out, it was believed that the 'black man' had conferred upon Temperance the ability to become invisible; for Anne Wakely and several other women were in the chamber, but unable to see either Temperance or the black man himself.

On the 30th of June, the black man appeared to Temperance near her own door and again tempted her to go to Thomas Eastchurch's house to 'make an end' of Grace Thomas. She and the black man again entered her chamber where Temperance pinched and pricked Grace upon several parts of her body. The black man,

Temperance is said to have confessed, promised her 'that no one should discover her or see her'.

Then, at midnight, the black man 'did suck her in the street in her secret parts, she kneeling down to him' and afterwards he 'vanished clear away out of her sight'. He was described as wearing 'blackish clothes' and that in height Temperance said he was 'about the length of her arm'. His eyes were broad and his mouth like that of a toad.

As was quite usual in cases of witchcraft accusation, Temperance Lloyd was 'searched' whilst in the lock-up by a number of the townswomen. Such an examination would have been an extremely invasive and degrading affair, in which any blemish or bump, no matter how slight, could be taken as a witch's mark; signifying one of the Devil's own, or a witch's teat; there for the purpose of suckling the Devil and familiar spirits.

Upon Temperance's body, the townswomen found what they took to be two 'teats' in her privy parts; each about an inch long. One of the women who searched her, Anne Wakely, questioned Temperance as to whether she had suckled the 'black man' with these teats, to which she replied she had, and that this had last happened on the 30th of June.

The following day, on Monday the 3rd of July, statements were given by Thomas and Elizabeth Eastchurch, Grace Thomas, Anne Wakely and Honor Hooper. Temperance was questioned by the justices, and admitted all the accusations made against her.

On the Tuesday, Temperance faced further questioning. She was taken to the parish church and there questioned by the rector Michael Ogilby. Again, she admitted each of the accusations put to her. On the question of image magic, Temperance confessed to having fetched from Thomas Eastchurch's shop a 'puppet or picture' (a doll) on the 23rd of June, and that she 'left it about the bed' of Grace Thomas. However, she denied that she had 'prickt any pins in the said puppet', and would not reveal where in the house or in what part of the bed she had left the puppet, for if she did the 'Devil would tear her in pieces.'

She was also questioned whilst in the lock-up in Bideford by William Herbert, the son of the William Herbert she was accused and acquitted of killing by witchcraft in 1671.

He demanded to know of her whether she had caused harm to his late father, as well as to Lydia Burman. She responded that indeed she had caused their deaths, and confessed also that she had caused the death of Anne Fellow, and to 'bewitching out one of the eyes' of the wife of Simon Dallyn, a mariner. When William asked why she had not confessed these crimes before, she responded that 'her time was not expired; for the Devil had given her greater power, and a longer time.' All of this information, Temperance also confessed to the justices upon questioning.

On Saturday the 8th of July, Temperance Lloyd was taken away to Exeter to await her trial in gaol.

Grace Barnes was struck with a violent seizure on the morning of Sunday the 16th. So extreme was the attack that 'four men and women could hardly hold her'. Agnes Whitefield, who was attending to grace Barnes during the seizure, heard someone outside the door. Upon opening the door, she found Mary Trembles 'standing with a whitepot in her hands, as though she had been going to the common bakehouse.'

Grace Barnes, despite the violence of her seizure, appeared to have the strength and awareness to enquire who it was at the door, and upon learning that it was Mary Trembles, she accused her, and Susannah Edwards (who she had already suspected) of bewitching her.

It was claimed by William Edwards, a Bideford blacksmith, that he heard Susannah Edwards make a confession the following day, although it is not explained where or why this took place. He claimed to hear her confess that the devil had carnal knowledge of her body, and that he had sucked her in her breast and in her secret parts.' And that 'she and Mary Trembles did appear hand in hand invisible in John Barnes's house' in order to 'make an end' of Grace Barnes.

Tuesday the 18th of July 1682 saw the arrest of Mary Trembles and Susannah Edwards. Apparently, a man named John Dunning from Torrington had visited and questioned Susannah Edwards, but bizarrely, despite supposedly receiving a full confession, he was not required to give a statement reporting what had been said. Instead, a Joan Jones gave a full statement detailing what she claimed to have overheard Susannah Edwards confess to John Dunning. Demanding to know how she had become a witch, it was claimed she responded that, when she was at one time gathering wood, a gentleman came to her in Parsonage Close and that she was in good hopes of having a little money from him.

Joan Jones then claimed that, after John Dunning left, she heard Edwards make further confessions (but just who these confessions were supposedly made to doesn't seem to have mattered). She confessed, it was claimed, that on July the 16th, she and Mary Trembles 'did prick and torment' Grace Barnes with the help of the Devil. Both Susannah Edwards and Mary Trembles then confessed that earlier that very day they had done the same again.

A small argument then broke out between the pair with Mary Trembles saying *'O thou rogue, I will now confess all: for it is thou that hast made me to be a witch, and thou art one thyself, and my conscience must swear it.'* To which Susannah replied *'I did not think that thou wouldst have been such a rogue to discover it.'*

She then went on to confess 'that the devil did oftentimes carry about her spirit', that she 'did prick and torment one Dorcas Coleman', and that she 'was sucked in her breast several times by the devil in the shape of a boy lying beside her in the bed; and that it was very cold unto her' and 'after she was sucked by him, the said boy or Devil had the carnal knowledge of her body four several times.'

Joan then related an incident that was supposed to have occurred that day in the guildhall during Susannah's questioning. Her husband, Anthony Jones, had observed Susannah 'to gripe and twinkle her hands upon her own body', upon which he said to her *Thou Devil, thou art now tormenting some person or other'*, to which Susannah was said to have responded *'Well enough, I will fit thee.'*

A constable was then sent with Joan's husband and others to fetch Grace Barnes (who at that time was suffering terrible pains) to the hall. When they returned, Susannah 'looked upon' Anthony whereupon he cried out 'Wife, I am now bewitched by this Devil' and then 'leapt and capered like a madman, and fell a shaking, quivering, and foaming, and lay for the space of half an hour like a dying or dead man'. This dramatic account would later be repeated, the following day, in a statement given by Anthony Jones himself.

In Mary trembles examination on the 18th, she was questioned as to how long she had practised witchcraft. She confessed that three years previously, Susannah Edwards had said to her that if she would do as she herself did then she 'should do very well' and promised that she 'should neither want for money, meat, drink, nor clothes.' After, the Devil 'in the shape of a lyon' came to her and had 'carnal knowledge of her body.' He then 'did suck her in her secret parts, and his sucking was so hard, which caused her to cry out for the pain thereof.'

She then gave an account of her and Susannah Edwards' unsuccessful attempt to beg food and tobacco from Grace Barnes on Easter Tuesday, before confessing that on the 16th, she and Susannah had gone to John Barnes's house 'and went at the fore-door invisibly into the room, where they did pinch and prick the said Grace Barnes almost unto death.'

Being asked upon how many other occasions the Devil had had 'the carnal knowledge of her body', Mary confessed that 'the Devil hath had the carnal knowledge of her body three other times.' The last of these occasions was on the 16th, when she had been on her way to the bakehouse, and 'at that time she, with the help of the Devil, would have killed the said Grace Barnes' if she had not spilt some of the meat she was carrying.

The examination of Susannah Edwards, which confusingly is incorrectly stated in the records to have taken place on the 10th of July, gives details of her first encounter with the Devil.

She confessed that two years previously, she had met a gentleman, dressed all in black, in a field named Parsonage Close. She was hopeful of begging some money from him. As the gentleman drew near, 'she did make a curchy or courtesie unto him, as she did use to do to gentlemen.' When asked who the gentleman was, she responded that he was the Devil.

The Devil asked Susannah if she was a poor woman; she responded that indeed she was. The Devil then promised that if she would grant him one request, then 'she should neither want for meat, drink, nor clothes.' Susannah exclaimed *'In the Name of God, what is it that I shall have?'* and the Devil vanished immediately from sight.

Susannah confessed also that, following this encounter, 'something in the shape of a little boy, which she thinks to be the Devil, came into her house and did lie with her, and that he did suck her at her breast.'

Her next meeting with the Devil took place in 'Stambridge-lane' where 'he did suck blood out of her breast.'

She repeated Mary Trembles' confession that they had both gone to John Barnes house on the 16th and invisibly tormented his wife by pinching and pricking her. The traditional witch skill of spirit travel is spoken of when Susannah then explained that 'she can go unto any place invisible, and yet her body shall be lying in her bed.'

Her examiners asked if she had done harm by witchcraft to any person other than Grace Barns, to which she confessed that 'she did prick and torment one Dorcas Coleman.

A form of hierarchy was revealed in her explanation to her examiners that Mary Trembles was a servant to her 'in like manner as she this examinant was a servant unto the Devil.'

Their examinations over, and their confessions made, Mary Trembles and Susannah Edwards were taken away from Bideford to Join Termerance Lloyd in Exeter Gaol, there to await trial.

Further statements would be made by Dorcas and John Coleman, and Thomas Bremincorn on the 26th of July, Grace Barnes on the 2nd of August, and William Herbert on the 12th of August.

The statements of Dorcas Coleman, Thomas Bremincorn and John Coleman related the incident of Dorcas becoming ill with pricking pains at the end of August 1680, and Dr Beare being brought by Thomas Bremincorn to see her who then diagnosed witchcraft to be the cause of her suffering.

Dorcas also related that at the time of her suffering she would see Susannah Edwards in her chamber, and that she would 'point with her finger at what place in the chamber the said Susannah Edwards would stand, and where she would go.'

In their statements, Thomas Bremincorn and John Coleman both told of an incident that occurred when Susannah Edwards had come to visit Dorcas in her chamber. Thomas's version, which was closely repeated by John's, relates that 'as soon as the said Dorcas did see the said Susannah Edwards, she did strive to fly in the face of the said Susannah; but was not able to get out of the chair wherein she sat. This informant, and John Coleman the said Dorcas's husband, did strive to help her out of the chair: upon which the said Susannah Edwards began to go backwards for to go out of the chamber.'

Dorcas's striving to 'fly in the face of the said Susanna' may possibly have been an attempt at 'scoring above the breath', in which a supposed victim of witchcraft would attempt to draw blood, often from the forehead of the suspected witch, in order to lift the influence of the spell and to nullify the witch's power. Such an antidote to ill-wishing was widely known and used in the West Country.

Grace Barns, in her statement, spoke of the tormenting pains she had suffered, and described how she had sought far and wide for a remedy, and that she had never suspected a magic or witchcraft as the cause for her suffering until she had been 'informed by some physicians that it was so.'

Armed with this information, her suspicions then fell upon Susannah Edwards because she 'would oftentimes repair unto this informant's husband's house upon frivolous or no occasions at all.'

Grace spoke also of the incident in which Mary Trembles had been at her door while 'she was taken in a very grievous and tormenting manner' causing her suspicion to fall upon Mary also.

William Herbert's statement related the confessions he claimed to have received from Temperance Lloyd whilst she was held in Bideford lock-up.

The trial of Temperance Lloyd, Susannah Edwards and Mary Trembles took place at Exeter Castle on the 14th of August, 1682.

Following the trial, Lord Chief Justice Sir Francis North wrote a letter to Secretary of State Sir Leoline Jenkins describing the occasion as related to him by Sir Thomas Raymond, the judge who presided over the trial;

'Here have been three old women condemned for witchcraft. Your curiosity will make you enquire of their circumstances. I shall only tell you what I had from my brother Raymond, before

whom they were tried, that they were the most old, decrepid, despicable, miserable creatures that ever he saw. A painter would have chosen them out of the whole country for figures of that kind to have drawn by. The evidence against them was very full and fanciful, but their own confessions exceeded it. They appeared not only weary of their lives but to have a great deal of skill to convict themselves. Their description of sucking devils with saucer eyes were so natural that the jury could not choose but believe them. I find the country so fully possessed against them that, though some of the virtuosi may think these things the effects of confederacy, melancholy or delusion and that young folks are altogether as quicksighted as they who are old and infirm, yet we cannot reprieve them without appearing to deny the very being of witches, as it is contrary to the law, so I think it would be ill for his Majesty's service, for it may give the faction occasion to set afoot the old trade of witch finding, that may cost many innocent persons their lives, which this justice will prevent.'

Roger North, who was present at the trial, wrote of it in his biography of his brother Sir Francis North:

'The women were very old, decrepit, and impotent, and were brought to the assizes with as much noise and fury of the rabble against them as could be shewed on any occasion. The stories of their arts were in everyone's mouth, and they were not content to belie them in the country, but even in the city where they were to be tried miracles were fathered upon them, as that the judge's coach was fixed upon the castle bridge, and the like. All which the country believed, and accordingly persecuted the wretched old creatures. A less zeal in a city or kingdom hath been the overture of defection or revolution, and if these women had been acquitted, it was thought that the country people would have committed some disorder.'

These accounts reveal the disbelief in witchcraft that was by that time rapidly spreading amongst the social elite, but also that this was in stark contrast to the old witch beliefs still fervently held onto by the common populace. Great unrest would have been the likely result of an innocent verdict, made all the more difficult by the complete willingness of the three women to confess to all accusations put to them, and so they were found guilty and removed again to Exeter Gaol to await their executions.

On Friday the 25th of August, a large crowd gathered to witness the deaths of the Bideford witches. The occasion and the last words of the condemned women were recorded.

'The substance of the last words and confessions of Susanna Edwards, Temperance Lloyd, and Mary Trembles, at the time and place of their execution; as fully as can be taken in a case liable to so much noise and confusion, as is usual on such occasions.

Mr. H. *Mary Trembles, what have you to say as to the crime you are now to die for?*

Mary. *I have spoke as much as I can speak already, and can speak no more.*

H. *In what shape did the Devil come to you?*

Mary. *The Devil came to me once, I think, like a lyon.*

H. *Did he offer any violence to you?*

Mary. *No, not at all, but did frighten me, and did nothing to me. And I cried to God, and asked what he would have, and he vanished.*

H. *Did he give thee any gift, or didst thou make him any promise?*

Mary. *No.*

H. *Did he have any of thy bloud?*

Mary. *No*

H. *Did he come to make use of thy body in a carnal manner?*

Mary. *Never in my life.*

H. *Have you a teat in your privy-parts?*

Mary. *None*

The Grand Inquest said it was sworn to them.

H. *Mary Trembles, was not the Devil there with Susan when I was once in prison with you, and under her coats? The other told* *me that he was there, but is now fled; and that the Devil was in the way when I was going to Taunton with my son who is a Minister. Thou speakest now as a dying woman, and as the Psalmist says, I will confess my iniquities and acknowledge all my sin. We find that Mary Magdalen had seven devils, and she came to Christ and obtained mercy: and if thou break thy league with the Devil, and make a Covenant with God, thou mayst also obtain mercy. If thou hast any thing to speak, speak thy mind.*

Mary. *I have spoke the very truth, and can speak no more: Mr. H. I would desire they may come by me, and confess as I have done.*

H. *Temperance Lloyd, have you made any contact with the Devil?*

Temp. *No*

H. *Did he ever take any of thy bloud?*

Temp. *No*

H. *How did he appear to thee first, or where in the street? In what shape?*

Temp. *In a woful shape.*

H. *Had he ever any carnal knowledge of thee?*

Temp. *No, never.*

H. *What did he do when he came to thee?*

Temp. *He caused me to go and do harm.*

H. *And did you go?*

Temp. *I did hurt a woman sore against my conscience: he carried me up to her door, which was open: the woman's name was Mrs. Grace Thomas.*

H. *What caused you to do her harm? what malice had you against her? Did she do you any harm?*

Temp. *No, she never did me any harm: but the Devil beat me about the head grievously because I would not kill her: but I did bruise her after this fashion [laying her two hands to her sides.]*

H. *Did you bruise her till the bloud came out of her mouth and nose?*

Temp. *No.*

H. *How many did you destroy and hurt?*

Temp. *None but she.*

H. *Did you know any mariners that you or your associates destroyed by overturning of ships and boats?*

Temp. *No; I never hurt any ship, bark, or boat in my life.*

H. *Was it you or Susan that did bewitch the children?*

Temp. *I sold apples, and the child took an apple from me, and the mother took the apple from the child; for the which I was very angry: but the child died of the Small Pox.*

H. *Do you know one Mr. Lutteril about these parts, or any of your confederates? Did you or them bewitch his child?*

Temp. *No.*

H. *Temperance, how did you come in to hurt Mrs. Grace Thomas? Did you pass through the key-hole of the door, or was the door open?*

Temp. *The Devil did lead me up the stairs, and the door was open: and this is all the hurt I did.*

H. *How do you know it was the Devil?*

Temp. *I knew it by his eyes?*

H. *Had you no discourse or treaty with him?*

Temp. *No; he said I should go along with him to destroy a woman, and I told him I would not: he said he would make me; and the Devil beat me about the head.*

H. *Why had you not called upon God?*

Temp. *He would not let me do it.*

H. *You say you never hurted ships nor boats; did you never ride over an arm of the sea on a cow?*

Temp. *No, no, master, 'twas she, meaning Susan.*

When Temperance said 'twas Susan, she said she lied, and that she was the cause of her bringing to die: for she said when she was first brought to gaol, if that she was hanged, she would have me hanged too; she reported I should ride on a cow before her, which I never did.

H. *Susan, did you see the shape of a bullock? At the first time of your examination you said it was like a short black man, about the length of your arm.*

Sus. *He was black sir.*

H. *Susan, had you any knowledge of the bewitching of Mr. Lutteril's child, or did you know a place called Tranton Burroughs.*

Sus. *No.*

H. *Are you willing to have any prayers?*

Then Mr. H. prayed, whose prayer we could not take; and they sung part of the 40 Psalm, at the desire of Susanna Edwards: as she mounted the ladder, she said, The Lord Jesus speed me; though my sins be as red as scarlet, the Lord Jesus can make them as white as snow; The Lord help my soul. Then she was executed.

Mary Trembles said, Lord Jesus receive my soul; Lord Jesus speed me; and then was also executed.

Temperance Lloyd said, Jesus Christ speed me well: Lord forgive all my sins; Lord Jesus Christ be merciful to my poor soul.

Mr. Sheriff. *You are lookt on as the woman that has debauched the other two: did you ever lie with Devils?*

Temp. *No.*

Sh. *Did not you know of their coming to gaol?*

Temp. *No.*

Sh. *Have you anything to say to satisfie the world?*

Temp. *I forgive them, as I desire the Lord Jesus Christ will forgive me. The greatest thing I did was to Mrs. Grace Thomas; and I desire I may be sensible of it, and that the Lord Jesus Christ may forgive me. The Devil met me in the street, and bid me kill her; and because I would not, he beat me about the head and back.*

Mr. Sh. *In what shape or colour was he?*

Temp. *In black, like a bullock.*

Sh. *How do you know you did it? How went you in, through the key-hole, or the door?*

Temp. *At the door.*

Sh. *Had you no discourse with the Devil?*

Temp. *Never but this day six weeks.*

Sh. *You were charged about 12 years since, and did you never see the Devil but this time?*

Temp. *Yes, once before: I was going for brooms, and he came to me and said, this poor woman has a great burthen; and would help ease me of my burthen: and I said, the Lord had enabled me to carry it so far, and I hope I shall be able to carry it further.*

Sh. *Did the Devil never promise you any thing?*

Temp. *No, never.*

63

Sh. *Then you have served a very bad master, who gave you nothing. Well, consider you are just departing this world: do you believe there is a God?*

Temp. *Yes.*

Sh. *Do you believe in Jesus Christ?*

Temp. *Yes; and I pray Jesus Christ to pardon all my sins. And so was executed.*

And so departed the souls of Susannah Edwards, Mary Trembles and Temperance Lloyd, the last people known to have been executed for witchcraft in England.

The memory of the three old Bideford witches however lingered long into the folklore of the area, and a tradition arose that they had shared together an old thatched cottage which burnt down in 1894.

The place was said to be haunted by their spirits, and there are many who are said to have seen them there, along with the Devil. One witness is said to have seen the witches gathered around an old crock when the Devil, with a spiked tail and cloven hooves, appeared and gave them something which they stirred into the pot. He then gave something 'bright' to each of the witches before disappearing back into the trees.

Susannah Edwards then did say '*Thrice the brindled cat hath mewed,*' and the three witches cackled wildly and then together began to chant:

> '*Beat the water, Trembles's daughter*
> *Till the tempest gather o'er us;*
> *Till the thunder strike with wonder,*
> *And the lightning flash before us!*
> *Beat the water, Trembles's daughter,*
> *Ruin seize our foes, and slaughter!*'

CECIL WILLIAMSON
A Modern Cunning Man

ecil Hugh Williamson (1909-1999), is a hugely important yet relatively overlooked, unrecognised, and all too often unheard of figure in the modern witchcraft revival. He was the founder of what is today named 'The Museum of Witchcraft & Magic' which began its life on the Isle of Man, eventually settling in the Cornish harbour village of Boscastle where it remains today. The founding of this world famous museum however is often incorrectly attributed to Gerald B. Gardner who, by complete contrast, is arguably modern witchcraft's most recognised and celebrated figure.

Cecil was born in Paignton, Devon, to well-to-do parents with whom he appears not to have enjoyed a particularly close relationship; growing up in boarding schools and often holidaying with other relatives. It was during one such holiday, with his uncle in Devonshire's North Bovey that his first encounter with the world of witchcraft occurred and is described in this present book's introduction.

At his boarding school in Buckinghamshire, the young Cecil Williamson experienced a direct encounter with witchcraft for a second time. He was being cruelly bullied by a boy he names in some accounts as 'Balstrode', and it was in hiding from this tormentor, one day amongst the trees, that he was first introduced to the actual working of magic. He was found by a woman, who appears to have worked in the school kitchens, who enquired why Cecil was looking so unhappy. Upon hearing of his problems, she taught the young Cecil how to perform a spell that would rid him of his bully. She took out a small portable swing, hung it from a strong tree branch and directly beneath it she built a small fire. Cecil was instructed to climb upon the device and swing to and fro through the fire's rising smoke whilst intoning repeatedly; *'Balstrode away, Balstrode away'* for no less than twenty minutes. If Cecil repeated this spell each day throughout the holidays, then he would no longer receive any bother from Balstrode.

Needing a suitable place to perform his magic whilst home for the holidays, Cecil was fortunate to come by a friendly game keeper who agreed to humour the boy, and help him build a fire and set up a swing from a suitable tree in the dog cemetery in Hyde Park. So here Cecil continued his spell for twenty minutes each day until the holidays were over.

Upon returning to school, Cecil was amazed to find that not only was Balstrode absent, but that he would never be returning as he had suffered a serious skiing accident which had left the boy a cripple. Such a striking incident would have most likely impressed vividly upon young Cecil's mind the efficacy and reality of magic and witchcraft, sealing further his interests in this most extraordinary and ancient facet of life.

The world of magic would be next encountered in the unlikely setting of East London's impoverished Docklands area, when Cecil Williamson, as a student volunteer, was helping out with a charitable soup kitchen. Here, Cecil again encountered the wise women and cunning men, working their operative magic for the needs of those in their community.

Whilst in London, and later when staying in France with his Grandmother, Cecil Williamson also encountered, and had first-hand experience of the very different world of high society ceremonial occultism, with its elaborate and often bizarrely disturbing rituals. Such experiences are sure to have left a lasting impression on Cecil, for although he maintained an interest in Ceremonial magic, giving it space within his museums, and even experimenting with it in his own work, it seems Cecil was largely suspicious and fairly dismissive of elaborate, organised and rigid systems of magic, and especially of their associated closed societies and groups. Such things were far removed from the operative magic of what he would come to call the 'wayside witches', whose direct work with the world of 'spirit force' formed the core of his lifelong fascination.

After ill-fated attempts to begin careers in the Navy, and then the Church, Cecil found himself being sent off to work on a tobacco plantation in Rhodesia (now Zimbabwe). Yet again, there in that strange and distant land, magic was never far from him and persisted in finding its way into Cecil's life. His time in Rhodesia seems to have been a difficult episode in his life,[15] but

---

15. Patterson, Steve. *Cecil Williamson's Book of Witchcraft*, p.126-127.

comfort was drawn from his friendship there with his 'house boy', a retired witch doctor named Zandonda. Through Zandonda and his 'brother craftsmen', Cecil would encounter a form of magic from which he was able to learn 'a wealth of magical skill and knowhow', and yet was, at the same time, so familiar and reminiscent of the ways of the wise woman and 'wayside witches' of home.

Upon returning to Britain, Cecil experienced a rather extreme change of scene when he became involved with the film industry, and with some success; at least one movie directed by him is still available today. It was in this more glamorous period of his life that Cecil encountered a good number of the 'big names' of the occult world, including 'The Great Beast' Aleister Crowley, Dr Margaret Murray and Montague Summers.

Eventually, through a family friend, who also happened to be brother-in-law to the famous occultist and writer Dion Fortune, Cecil became involved with MI6 and the covert monitoring of the rumoured occult interests and activities within the German government, and its military. Thus began 'The Witchcraft Research Centre' which Cecil would continue to operate for the rest of his life, and which would run as a separate but parallel entity to his later witchcraft museums.

As well as his covert investigative work, Cecil was also involved in the disseminating of propaganda and disinformation to the Germans; work which necessitated the setting up of radio installations, one of which was in the New Forest. It was here that Cecil met Mrs. Edith Woodford-Grimes, who would again feature in his life via his not always amicable involvement with Gerald B. Gardner, which subsequently began as a result of the two men meeting in London's famous Atlantis Bookshop in 1947.[16]

16. Patterson, Steve. *Cecil Williamson's Book of Witchcraft*, p.130.

The two men of course shared a keen interest in the modern survival of witchcraft practices and traditions, albeit with differing views on the nature of the Craft, and it was around this time that Cecil Williamson was exploring plans to open a museum devoted to the subject.

In his study and exploration of the 'silent world of witchcraft', Cecil was steadily amassing a collection of artefacts, stories and practices relating to the modern-day practitioners of traditional, and often idiosyncratic ways of magic; with a particular focus upon the what he called the 'wayside witches' of Devon, Cornwall and Somerset.

Cecil made his first, but unsuccessful attempt to establish his museum in Stratford-on-Avon in 1947, when a local doctor had granted him the use of a, by then, disused fire engine garage. It had been built in his garden when it had been requisitioned during the war.[17]

As soon as he opened his exhibition however, he faced such fierce local opposition to the displaying of witchcraft that he found himself run out of town. Thankfully, Cecil was quite determined to achieve his goal, and found another location for his museum on the Isle of Man. There he purchased the derelict mill buildings known as the 'Witches' Mill' due to a local legend that a coven of Manx witches used to meet there to perform their magical rites. Certainly, there are other cases of the association between old mills and witches.

Cecil set about renovating a portion of the buildings and, coinciding with the repeal of the Witchcraft Act in 1951, opened his museum as 'The Folklore Centre of Superstition & Witchcraft'.[18]

Here, the museum was successfully established, apparently free of any serious opposition, and even included its own on-site restaurant called 'The Witches Kitchen', which was run by Cecil's wife Gwen.

---

17. Howard, Michael. *West Country Witches*, p.100.
18. *Ibid. The Cauldron* No. 95, p.5.

Having heard of the museum's opening and keen to be involved, a rather dishevelled Gerald Gardner, down on his financial luck, travelled to the Isle of Man and turned up on the Williamsons' doorstep, carrying an old music case containing his pyjamas and toothbrush. Cecil found a small cottage on the island for Gardner, and allowed him to offer unsold copies of his book '*High Magic's Aid*' for sale in the museum restaurant.

Another figure, soon to become a vital part of the modern witchcraft movement, had also learned of the museum's opening through reading an article in *Illustrated*. Doreen Valiente related in her book '*The Rebirth of Witchcraft*' that before coming by this article 'I had never had any real reason to believe that the witch cult was still active in Britain, or that I could contact it'. Seeking more information, Doreen wrote to Cecil Williamson, who passed her enquiry onto Gerald Gardner, who subsequently invited her to meet with him at the home of Edith Woodford-Grimes, or 'Dafo' as she was known, in the Christchurch area. The following summer she was initiated by Gerald as a witch, and the rest, as they say, is history.[19]

Living in each other's pockets on the Isle of Man did little for Cecil and Gerald's friendship, and the relationship quickly began to sour; perhaps not helped by the fact that the two men had very differing views on the nature of witchcraft. Gerald Gardner's vision was for the establishment of witchcraft as a pagan fertility religion for the masses, with a focus upon ritual celebration and the worship of goddesses and gods within organised initiatory coven structures. To him the museum was an ideal publicity machine for his recruitment drive, and tensions arose surrounding the prominence he sought to give the display of 'New Forest' witch artefacts.

For Cecil, on the other hand, witchcraft was the magical arte and craft of the 'wayside' practitioner;

---

19. Valiente, Doreen. *The Rebirth of Witchcraft*, P.36-40.

operating for the most part on a solitary basis and gaining their knowledge and power via a direct and deeply personal working relationship with the spirit world. This vision of magical, results-based witchcraft was for the few, and Cecil held firmly to the opinion that one could not work effective witchcraft without first attaining a working relationship with a familiar spirit. In various articles, Cecil writes of his surprise and frustration that Gerald Gardner showed no interest in the concept of the familiar spirit, despite its central position within the lore of British witchcraft and folk-magic, and it remains curiously absent within the established traditions of Wicca.

For Cecil, the reason for this lack of interest lay in the simple fact that Gerald was really rather afraid of the whole idea of spirits. To illustrate this, Cecil delights in giving an account of an incident involving an impressive incense burner in his possession, which if used in a certain way with a circle of candles in a draught free room, would cause columns of smoke to arise and take on uncannily humanoid forms. Cecil confesses;

'So I put on a show for Gardner. I asked if he had any pet spirits he wanted to call up. "Oh, yes, yes" he said. So he came along, all dressed up in his gear and he had got his sandals on with his toes sticking out and all the rest of it. And he'd got his wand and he'd got his sword and he'd got his script and he'd got his lectern. And he started off, banging away there, running through all his names and the room was getting fuller and fuller of smoke. Bless his heart, he suffered from asthma so he did start coughing a bit but, give him his due, he had his script there and everything was proceeding and the candles were going and it was warm and the smoke was going and he was in full song and he went on, and then... all of a sudden, he looked up and there was what just looked like a person in a blessed hood! He took one look at it and cried "Good God!" and he was off!' [20]

---

20. *Talking Stick*, Autumn 1992, p.20.

Whilst it must of course have been an unpleasant episode for all concerned at the time, I am sure a comedy could be written about Cecil and Gerald in their witchcraft museum and the degeneration of their relationship; which appears to have come to a head with Gerald lunging at Cecil in anger with an athame!

Eventually, Cecil decided it was time to move on; he sold the 'Witches' Mill' buildings to Gerald, loaning him some of his artefacts, and returned with his museum to England, setting up first in Windsor. It was here, with his 'Witchcraft Exhibition' that he met one of the many 'old style' witches who would teach him something of their ways. He gives her name as Rosa Woodman, 'The Royal Witch of Windsor', who it seems fulfilled a role as some kind of magical protector of the royal household. Cecil, she was certain, was the right person to become her successor. She taught him a divinatory ritual, involving lengthy dances and the throwing of a witches' rosary of 99 acorns, not far from the site of 'Herne's Oak' in Windsor Great Park. Upon Rosa's passing, this magical rosary was bequeathed to Cecil, along with her familiar; a toad named Tim, and her magical 'turning stick', a naturally twisted walking stick named 'Sticky'.

It appears that Cecil was not up to the job of keeping and caring for a toad familiar, and so he found a suitable new home for Tim inside an old table top tomb in a graveyard. The rosary of 99 acorns seems to have vanished without a trace, but the 'turning sick' remained with Cecil for the rest of his life. Upon Cecil's death in 1999, the stick was passed to Cecil's friend, the West Country witch Brownie Pate, and upon her passing Sticky returned, along with a number of Brownie's other magical items and note books, to the museum where it remains on display.

Also, while exhibiting his collection in Windsor, Cecil was visited by two men who it seems were royal officials, who politely but firmly explained that Windsor might

The village green at North Bovey

A Devonshire 'Village Wise Man'
photographed in Devonshire Characters & Strange Events, 1908.

The large 'steen' in which Ann, the Toad Witch of North Bovey, kept her toads. Photographed in Devon & Cornwall Notes & Queries, 1901.

The Devonshire witch Mariann Voaden and her collapsed cottage
Photographs from Devonshire Characters & Strange Events, 1908.

West Country witch tools in the Museum of Witchcraft & Magic. 'Old Martha Whitchalse's brazen cauldron' along with an 'egg wand' from Umberleigh, and a 'spell stone' from Yarcombe. Below: the Bideford Witches Memorial.

THE DEVON WITCHES
IN MEMORY OF
Temperance Lloyd
Susannah Edwards
Mary Trembles
OF BIDEFORD DIED 1682
Alice Molland
DIED 1685
THE LAST PEOPLE IN ENGLAND
TO BE EXECUTED FOR WITCHCRAFT
TRIED HERE & HANGED AT HEAVITREE
In the hope of an end to persecution & intolerance

Cecil Williamson using image magic to perform a counter-curse.

Cecil Williamson's home in the North Devon village of Witheridge.
Below: witch bottles from Plymouth in the Museum of Witchcraft & Magic.

Human skull spirit houses used in Devon. Below: a pig skull prepared as a protection charm by a Cullompton witch, and once used by Gerald Gardner in ritual. The Horse skull housed 'nightmare riding spirits' on a Drewsteignton farm. Cow bone and iron chain prepared by a Devon witch as a horse protection charm.

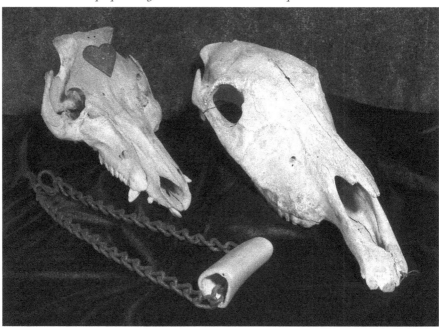

A spirit house made by a Honiton witch using a lace maker's globe filled with hundreds and thousands. It is said that the spirit housed within it 'could be quite nasty at times'. From the Museum of Witchcraft & Magic.

The Dewerstone – haunted by the Wild hunt and a Black Dog apparition. Below; Soussons Common Circle where, in 1903, evidence of witchcraft was unearthed when a carefully buried lock of hair was discovered at its centre.

Scorhill Circle on Gidleigh Common;
Below: the Tolmen stone, used in curative folk magic and initiatory witch rites.

Spinsters Rock chamber tomb on Shilstone Farm, Drewsteignton.
Below; 'The Witches' Rock', Putts Corner, Sidbury.

'The Devil's Stone', Shebbear.

Wistman's Wood, Dartmoor, and Inky, the author's greyhound, demonstrating the appearance of a (rather handsome) wisht hound.

The tomb of Squire Cabell in Buckfastleigh churchyard.
Below: Granite altar kept by a witch on Bench Tor. Snake vertebrae necklace from
Collumpton, worn to 'confer upon the witch a degree of magical and spiritual power.'

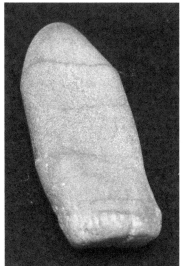
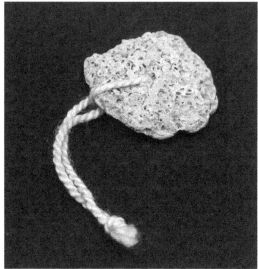

Stone carried against toothache, and stone on string used to cure warts. Both from South Devon. Clarke Collection. Below: Rings, made from half-crowns or florins featured in rites to cure seizures. Museum of Witchcraft & Magic.

not be a suitable home for such a collection, and that he should perhaps relocate. Being people with contacts, it was made clear to him that, to aid his relocation, certain strings could be pulled and Cecil would face no issues with planning etc.

And so Cecil and his museum were on the move again and reopened in the pretty Cotswolds village of Bourton-on-the-Water in 1956. This however was not a happy new home for the collection, as local Christians subjected Cecil to a barrage of persecution; including fire attacks on the museum and the hanging of a dead cat outside. The local vicar even refused to give communion to Cecil's housekeeper, and ranted against Cecil and his museum from the pulpit. When the vicar died not long after, suspicion must naturally have arisen that Cecil may have retaliated by magical means, an act Cecil himself neither confirmed nor denied![1]

At this time, Cecil owned property in Cornwall, and so retreated from Bourton-on-the-Water to set his museum up in the East Cornish town of Looe; naming it the 'House of Spells'. Again, however, the Christians of the area made it known that such a museum was not welcome and so Cecil was forced to make further relocations of the collection; first to Tintagel, where the museum seemed to be welcomed, but made little money, and again to nearby Boscastle. Not only was this beautiful little harbour village a popular tourist 'honey pot', but was said to have been home to working 'sea witches' who would sell the wind, magically tied into knotted rope, to sailors. The strange, numinous atmosphere of the village, its natural harbour, and its wooded valley have often been commented upon, and it is indeed a place that seems to hold a strange attraction for witches and occultists for it has been home to good number of such people, which I suspect would still be the case if the museum were not situated there.

---

1. Patterson, Steve. *Cecil Williamson's Book of Witchcraft*, p.136.

Finally, finding the perfect location for his collection, Cecil continued to run the museum in Boscastle, all the way through to 1996, when he sold it; passing the museum into the capable hands of Graham King.

I find it rather sad that Cecil Williamson seemed to feel he had failed in some way by having never written a book.[2] Of course, the type of witchcraft written about by his old associate Gerald Gardner went from being the pursuit of a few small groups in Britain to become a religion followed by countless people all around the world, all be it in a manner often very diluted from Gardner's original vision.

The form of witchcraft Cecil Williamson devoted his life to, by contrast, would seem in comparison to have slipped 'under the radar', but then it always was a way for the few; a way in which Cecil was fully active as a working witch in the old 'cunning' tradition. He was known to have worked for those who sought his help for such traditional matters as the lifting and returning of curses, and the recovery of lost or stolen property.

Despite having never written books on the subject, Cecil Williamson's influence and his importance to the world of witchcraft is great indeed. His life's work has left a world famous collection of artefacts viewed, I believe, by more than 50000 people per year. The artefacts themselves, his accompanying hand typed description cards, his body of articles and his archived correspondence, culminate to reveal a very different and very potent world of real, hands-on witchcraft and magic that works 'hand in glove' with the silent world of spirit. Time and time again one hears of or encounters witches and occultists whose work has been directly inspired by Cecil Williamson and his Museum of Witchcraft and Magic.

---

2. Patterson, Steve. *Cecil Williamson's Book of Witchcraft*, p.120.

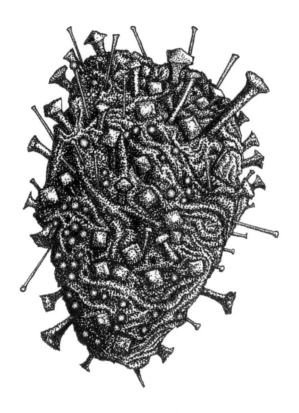

ENCOUNTERS *with* WITCHERY

ithin Devonshire's witch-lore there are to be found many accounts of the situations and circumstances that could arise when the worlds of the ordinary folk and the magical crossed, for good or ill. Most often, of course, when the results of such encounters were of the latter kind, they were more likely to have been recorded; when perhaps some manner of offense is seen to have been caused to one locally reputed to be a witch, and dire mishaps and misfortunes begin, uncannily, to occur.

The retaliation of the offended witch is illustrated in the story of The Witch and the Pin, which comes to us from 17th century Honiton. The servant girl of a successful draper was serving one Saturday at the haberdashery stall, set up outside of her master's door. An elderly woman, reputed locally to be a witch, approached the stall and asked the girl to give her a large pin from the selection displayed for sale. As the pins were not her property to give away, she instead pulled a pin of her own from her dress and kindly offered it to the woman. This offering was rejected, and the difficult old woman went off in a fury, muttering that the girl would soon regret her refusal to give her what she wanted. The next day, as she was serving her master's table during dinner, the girl let out a scream in pain, and exclaimed that someone had stuck her in the leg with a pin, although no one was near enough to do this to her at the time. Upon inspection, there was indeed a large pin stuck deep into her thigh. So deep was the pin that the girl had to be taken to Exeter to see a doctor for its removal.

Some suspected witches were so unpleasant in character however, that they were happy to exert their ill-influence on those they had simply taken a disliking to, without any apparent offence having been caused. One such witch once lived in the little village of Bucks Mills, and she was known to carry with her, as she stomped about the village in a temper, an old post-horn. With this, upon meeting someone she didn't like, or who had annoyed her in some minor way, she would blow a discordant blast of noise directly in her victim's face. One man, having received such a blast from the antisocial witch's horn, fell ill with a mysterious skin disease which took several months to bring under control. The doctor treating the man could not fathom the nature of the ailment, the likes of which he had never before seen.

Even such dark encounters however often reveal the recourse the ordinary folk had to witches of a more helpful inclination, and other practitioners of the magical artes. Accounts of this nature provide us with valuable insights into the magical modus operandi of rituals, spells and charms employed by the practitioner, or by their client under their instruction, to counteract the ill-influence of the disgruntled black witch.

Other accounts show the ways in which the help of magical folk might be sought to restore order when encounters with the spirit world cause everyday life to go awry, or to return lost or stolen property. But of curses and their lifting, the following story is a good example.

The Black Witch's Imp 🐾

A farming family, living on Dartmoor, appear to have caused some offence (it is not recorded how) to the local 'black witch' who in turn placed the 'evil eye' upon them. Twelve bullocks kept by the family, were all suddenly struck with a mysterious malady, and vets were called in, all manner of treatments tried, but none worked and none could discover the nature of their illness. The evil of the black witch was of course strongly suspected.

As the family sat in the farm cottage that night, discussing the deeply worrying implications of losing such valuable livestock, a most bizarre looking creature appeared within the chimney. It was described as something resembling a mixture of both a cat and a monkey, with scarlet fur, enormous eyes, a sinister grin, and dressed in a green hat and coat!

Pandemonium ensued as the otherworldly creature dashed from the chimney to wildly dance, caper, climb and leap about the cottage; knocking furniture and other possessions of the family flying, and always evading capture as they frantically chased the creature from room to room. After some time of this uproar, the creature mysteriously vanished through the locked door, leaving the poor family both exhausted and afraid.

The following day, the strange imp returned; this time riding on the backs of the farmer's sheep, causing them to run madly about the field until they fell in exhaustion. Again, in the evening, the imp appeared in the chimney, and so the farmer immediately went for his gun which he kept hung above the mantle, but as he did so, an unseen force struck the farmer; knocking him to the ground.

As the farmer fell, he grabbed the iron poker from the fireside, and struck out a mighty blow at the imp. However, not being of this world, the poker passed through the imp as if it were formed of mist. Again, the devilish creature careered from room to room causing a flurry of destruction as all manner of the family's things were thrown violently here and there, before vanishing just as it had done the night before.

When morning came, the misfortune continued as the farm's plough horse was struck, like the bullocks, with some mysterious disease. Knowing that the family were dealing with black workings of a spiritual nature, and that there was nothing else they could do, the farmer decided not to waste what little money he had left on vets, but instead set out to consult with a white witch.

The witch listened carefully to the farmer's story, and advised him to do the following. Upon his return to the farm, he was to gather enough whitethorn (hawthorn) to build a large fire, and procure a new bowl turned from ash wood. Into this bowl the farmer was to let some of the blood from one of his ailing bullocks; the animal chosen should be the one that appeared to be the sickest.

The fire of hawthorn was then to be lit, with the ashen bowl of blood placed at its centre. When the bowl split in the flames, the curse of the black witch would be lifted.

The farmer faithfully carried out the white witch's instructions, and sure enough, after the procedure had been completed, he inspected his bullocks to find them much improved in their condition, and heartily munching their hay. His plough horse recovered also, and his sheep, and indeed his home, were not bothered further by the mysterious imp who was never seen on the farm again.

The instructions of the white witch in this story are interesting, and have an air of authenticity about them. Indeed, whitethorn is traditionally associated in folk-magic with the spirit world, and the magic of calling upon or lifting its influence. The ash is of course a tree heavily associated with healing in traditional magic and with protection, and of course fire is a common ingredient in nearly all the needs for which folk-magic might be put into operation.

The blood is a most interesting part of this procedure, for it relates to the old magical belief that a part of the 'essence' of the 'black witch' and her power is present within her victim. This tradition provides a useful 'return path' direct to the witch within the work of curse lifting, and was often used also to cause suffering to the offending magic worker. We see it in the tradition of the witch bottle, where the influence of the black witch is thought to be present in the urine of the victim. This is heated in a fire, within the bottle, along often with other ingredients, to cause suffering to the witch and result in the lifting of the curse.

The selection of the sickest of the ailing animals in our story is possibly for the reason that this animal was likely to have been the first to have fallen victim to the ill-influence of the witch, or that in suffering more than the other animals, the presence of the witch's power was seen to be strongest within that animal, and so would provide the most potent 'return path' in destroying her influence.

By Fire and Fleas 🦋

A farmer from Torrington suspected the influence of black witchcraft had fallen upon his herd of cows when it began to suffer a spate of still-born calves. Upon consulting a local white witch his suspicion was duly confirmed. The black witch's identity was divined and revealed to the farmer, before instructions to lift the evil influence were given to him.

Upon returning home, the farmer was to take one of the still born calves to his hearth, and there hang it within the chimney above the fire, to be slowly burned away. The farmer was then, by stealth, to make his way into the house of the woman who had been revealed to him to be the black witch, and there, he was to catch three fleas from her bed and entrap them in a bottle by sealing it tightly with a cork. As long as the fleas remained within the bottle, kept by the farmer, and the calf's carcass remained hanging in the chimney to roast above the hearth-fire, the black witch would suffer strangury (a painful inability to pass water).

After a few days of this agony, the black witch would be compelled to pass by the farmer's house, peeping into the window as she goes. When this done, the spell would be lifted.

Again, within this story we find the witch's victim, in this case a still-born calf, employed as a means of return in order to punish the witch and negate her power. Often when witchcraft was the suspected cause of an animal's death, a more usual course of action was to remove its heart, stick it with pins, nails or thorns, and suspend it high within the chimney to slowly roast above the hearth fire. It is interesting in this case that the whole carcass instead was employed in this way. A bit dramatic perhaps, and a smouldering carcass can hardly be a pleasant thing to live with, but apparently effective none the less.

Sneaking into someone's home, to steal something intimately connected to a person in order to work magic upon them, is an act normally attributed to the 'black witch', but often in folk-magic, we find that the same methods employed by the ill-wisher may be used to defeat them. Fleas taken from someone's bed are of course highly intimate to the individual concerned, and therefor extremely useful in acts of sympathetic magic against them, but of course they are also highly likely to contain the witch's blood, having fed upon her in the night. Just as something of the witch was said to reside in the blood of her victim, so too was the witch's own blood seen to be the very seat of her power. Letting a witch's blood flow from her brow, or 'scoring above the breath' was an old and widespread method for nullifying her power.

The Beggar Witch 🌿

A Farm near Axminster was frequently visited by an old reputed witch, who lived nearby in a tiny cottage upon a wooded hill. She was able to live quite well on the food, supplies and money she incessantly begged from the farmer and his family. Quite naturally, they became fed up with the amount of hard worked for produce that was being handed over to the woman; especially when her tone was less than polite and she would demand rather than ask for aid. And so, it was decided that they would cut back on their generosity, and start refusing the woman aid on some of her visits. With this however, the woman's already limited aptitude for courtesy diminished further, and on each visit she would become more demanding and rude than ever before. On one such visit, demanding money from the farmer's usually gentle and kind brother, he refused and snapped at the old woman; reprimanding her for her manner, whereupon she stormed off in a foul temper, screeching that he'll have no need for his money much longer. Before three weeks had passed, the farmer's brother had fallen suddenly ill and died.

Any suspicion in the minds of the farmer's family that the woman was a witch were now confirmed, and the foolish woman had very definitely bitten the hand that fed her. Now, upon all her visits, the woman would be refused any aid whatsoever and turned away. One day, as the witch turned up, making her usual demands in vain, the farmer's young son was playing with a walnut which he offered up to the witch. His nurse intervened; taking the walnut from the child before the witch could lay her hands on it. Without uttering a word, she marked a circle with her gnarled old walking stick upon the ground around the child, marking also a cross inside it before storming off. That night, the poor child came down with an unknown illness; screaming with pain or fear, and within four days was dead.

Trouble and misfortune fell upon the house, with none of the household tasks, jobs or chores going as they should; anything and everything undertaken failed dramatically. One morning the farmer's wife was working in the pantry, when through the small window she spied the witch approaching the house. She told her maid to pretend to the old woman that she was not at home and to send her away. The girl opened the door, but before she could utter a word the witch shouted 'you can tell your mistress that until I permit so, she shall not set foot outside of that pantry of hers!' and again off she stomped. Just as the witch had said the farm mistress was unable to leave the pantry. No matter how hard she tried, nor how many helped to try and pull her out, she could not cross its threshold and had to remain there some hours, until finally she found she could leave.

Before the witch left the farm, nosing around, she found the horses being tended to in the stable and tried to beg some barley from their keeper. As all workers on the farm had been ordered though, he refused the woman. During the night, eight of the horses fell ill, and shortly after four of these were dead. Strange illnesses began to fall upon other animals, resulting in many deaths on an almost daily basis.

By now furious, and with no doubt that the old woman was the cause of the farm's misfortunes, the farmer took down his shotgun and made his way up the hill to the witch's cottage. There he confronted her, raising his gun, ready to take aim. The old woman fixed him with 'the witch's eye' and he was unable to move a muscle. It was obvious by now that the old woman's evil could not be thwarted by ordinary means, and so the farmer decided to travel to Chard where he would consult with a famous white witch.

After hearing of the farmer's troubles, the white witch consulted with his books, made his divinations, and announced to his desperate visitor that he and his farm were suffering from black witchcraft of the strongest kind, and that to lift its influence it would first be necessary for him to live there for a while and make further investigations. This process, he assured the farmer, would take no longer than one month; after which the farm should be free of injury.

Upon the white witch's arrival at the farm, the parlour was set aside as his 'work room' where he would be able to operate in private, behind the locked door with his books and magical apparatus. The farmer's family, and his staff were very curious about the wise man's workings, but from him they could get no details of his operations. Some nights he would disappear off to the dark wood where the witch's cottage stood. Other nights he would lock himself away in the parlour, consulting his books. On one such night, a servant girl couldn't resist the urge to spy through the key hole, whereupon she observed strange sparks of spirit light flying about the parlour as the white witch knelt in study before his old tomes.

Thankfully, some of the measures that had to be undertaken were not kept quite so occult, giving us an insight into some of the protections and counter magic the white witch of Chard employed. A large cauldron had to be kept boiling throughout the white witch's stay, with barley added to its water. This was to place the farm's surviving horses under protection from magical attack. Six bullock hearts, presumably taken from the bodies of animals that lay dead as a result of the ill-influence, were hung over the kitchen fire where they slowly smoked and smouldered. Four of these were stuck over with maiden nails (new nails that had never been allowed to touch the ground), and two were stuck with needles and pins.

The morning after the stuck hearts had been installed, the white witch informed the household that the old woman would come to the house claiming to be ill and begging food. He warned that that under no circumstances were they to offer any aid, for if they did, all that he had been able to accomplish would be undone, and her evil influence over the farm would double in potency. As the white witch had said, the old woman indeed called at the house, but although the farmer's wife felt some pity for the pathetic spectacle of a creature the formerly obnoxious woman had become, she held her ground and turned her away.

With three days remaining before the white witch's work would be complete, he took a large wooden barrel to the wooded hill, and there he drove many large iron nails into it. This device was then set to roll down the hill passing right by the tiny cottage of the black witch. Again, the white witch warned, in the morning, the old woman would visit the house and that her begging must be strictly refused. When morning came, so did the old woman, looking close to death, but again she was refused and turned away.

The following morning however, the old woman did not make an appearance at the farm, and the white witch went to the wood to investigate. There he found her window smashed, where she had been dragged out by the devil, and, high in a great old tree was her body; wrapped about with an old sheet and her kettle hanging from a branch beside her. So inaccessible was her body's situation that the tree had to be cut down in order to retrieve her remains. The witch's cottage was burnt to the ground; the locals being fearful that something of her influence might remain there. As it was set alight, her many cats dashed forth from the dark interior and disappeared deep into the wood.

After three days, the body of the black witch was buried at crossroads outside Axminster where her spirit, or her evil influence, seemed trapped; for horses would panic when passing the spot for years after her interment there. From the day of her death, the farm suffered no more mysterious misfortune and thrived. For his services, the white witch was paid £100.

An Unfortunate Family ✣

As we have seen, farmers seem to have had more than their fair share of trouble with witches, but one particular Devonshire farming family appears to have had the misfortune to receive the malevolent attentions of different black witches on three separate occasions. The stories are interesting for their illustration of Devonshire witch beliefs, and the methods employed to lift the influences of black witchcraft; for on each occasion, the aid of white witches was called upon.

As the eighteenth century was drawing to a close, a mid-Devonshire farm began to gather in its harvest. As was the practice in those days, most of the village arrived to help cut and bring in the corn in return for feasting and merriment; courtesy of the farmer's hospitality. One local family who turned up, the Bowdens, were not much welcome as they were not of pleasant character and long suspected of witchcraft. But on this occasion their presence was tolerated as every able hand was needed to get the work done.

The long and hard labours of the day being complete, all were gathered and merrily partaking of much cider and good food, when the father of the Bowdens threw his emptied plate rudely up the table to the farmer's wife for another helping. The plate broke; smashing others with it and the farmer's wife, angry at the man's clumsy incivility, snapped at him 'you witching old fool!' The

Bowden man immediately erupted into such a violent and pugnacious rage that a number of other harvesters had to take hold of him and, removed him from the house by force. Off he stomped from the farm, bellowing foul abuse to everyone, for it seems to be the nature of such belligerent people to blame everyone and anyone else for their fallouts rather than their own behaviour. Given the Bowden's reputation for witchcraft, there was a marked cloud of uneasiness over the remainder of the night's party; for fear of what might befall the farm as a result of the angry words of the farmer's wife.

The very next day, things did indeed begin to go very badly wrong for the farm. Every day, there were bizarre deaths amongst the livestock. The hens were struck down with a mysterious illness; preventing them from standing as if bones were broken, and the few eggs that were now being laid on the farm were soft shelled. Oxen were found dead in their stalls, one with a large set of harrows stuck about its horns, and two others found together in the same yoke. The farmer's riding horse was also found dead in the most inexplicable of circumstances. Before the animal could be unsaddled after returning from a journey to Crediton, it went missing. After a lengthy search, the dead body of the farmer's horse was eventually found in a local quarry; the unfortunate creature's hind and fore legs somehow having been passed both through the nearside stirrup. Neither fore nor hind hoof were small enough to have been passed through the stirrup by natural means, let alone the two together, and the two legs could only be extricated from their abstruse situation by the local blacksmith, who had to file the stirrup off.

The farmer was not one to believe in such things as witchcraft, the events on his farm however had left him with no option but to accept that witchcraft could be the only explanation. An urgent journey was made to consult with a white witch in Barnstaple. After listening intently to the farmer's terrible experiences, the white witch informed him that the influence of black witchcraft could be lifted from his farm by following his instructions carefully. The farmer was to return to his farm, where he would discover one last death within his livestock. The heart of this latest victim of ill-influence was to be cut from the creature's body and taken to the quarry where the body of the horse had been found. There, at nightfall, the farmer was to build and light a fire upon which to burn the heart; keeping vigil over it until the it had been reduced to ashes. During the performing of this rite, the farmer was told, a bleeding would occur somewhere on the farm, and some of the blood from this must be collected and brought to the white witch in order for the operation to be successfully completed.

Immediately, the farmer made his way back to the farm, searching amongst his remaining livestock for another death. Upon inspecting the calves, he found that one was obviously taken very ill, when suddenly it convulsed before him and died. Following carefully the white witch's instructions, he cut out the animal's heart, and took it to the quarry to burn upon a fire. Upon the completion of his vigil, he hurried back to the farm where he learned that one of his daughter's legs had mysteriously begun to bleed badly in her bed. The doctor was sent for and successfully stopped the bleed, and the girl recovered well; although her leg was never entirely right for the rest of her days. As instructed, the farmer delivered some of the blood unto the keeping of the white witch; presumably whose protective influence the farm was now under. The ill-influence did indeed seem to be lifted, and from that night the farm again prospered and was without trouble.

Many years after these events though, trouble returned to the farm at the hands of another witch-family. Two sisters, one of whom was widowed, and the husband of the other, lived together in a small cottage not far from the farm where they worked doing odd jobs and general maintenance. As was usual in those times, they were paid with produce from the farm, however, one 'settling day', when the widowed of the two sisters went to collect their share, she disputed the amount of produce the farmer's wife had given to her; claiming that her sister and brother-in-law were owed more. During the heated argument that arose from the dispute, a child playing beside the fire, fell over onto the hearth. Rushing to pick up the child before it suffered injury, the farmer's wife, knowing well that the widow and her family were suspected locally of having dealings with the Devil, screamed at the woman accusing her of witching the child into the fire. The widow stormed off screaming in return, 'before three months have passed, you'll know if I'm a witch or no!' Within three months, terrible troubles had returned once more to the farm, and livestock again began to die mysteriously, and in large numbers, until over £500 worth were gone.

The farmer who now ran the farm was a devout Christian, and refused to believe in the existence of witchcraft. However, his predecessor and relative, who had run the farm during its previous bewitchment, begged and pleaded with him to take the matter of ill-wishing seriously and to consult a white witch. When eventually he agreed, the two men travelled to Tiverton to consult with a white witch living there.

Upon entering the witch's home, and before either of the two men had spoken of their troubles, the white witch said unto them 'only now that your farm is near its ruin do you come to me! I could have stopped the troubles long before had only you come to see me sooner!' The witch took himself away to consult with his books and his spirits before giving instruction to his two visitors. 'Return home' – he said unto them – 'and on your way you will see the three black witches who have ill-wished you; for they will jump out before you on the path disguised in the form of hares. When you reach the farm, the very next of your animals to die must have its heart taken out. You must stick this heart over with very many pins before the whole thing is salted and buried in the ground.'

The two men returned for home, and just as the white witch had told them, three large hares emerged from drainage holes beside the lane and capered about a little distance before them, for about half a mile, before disappearing again into the hedges. Upon their return to the farm, the two men carried out the white witch's instructions faithfully, and immediately the deaths ceased and the farm began to recover.

One last time, however, our hapless farming family was to fall under the ill-influence of yet another witch family. One of the daughters of the farmer who had been bewitched by the Bowdens in the first story, had married a farmer who worked land on the other side of the village. An old woman in the village was at that time widely reputed to be a black witch, and none of the farms in the area would have any dealings with her, and would refuse to sell to her any of their produce. This was in accordance with a belief that to enter into dealings with a black witch was a dangerous thing; for it opened the way for them to exercise their powers over you.

However, the farmer one day walked into his kitchen to find his wife in the process of selling butter and eggs to the old witch. The woman was ordered out of his house and off the farm, and so she left; mumbling something under her breath as she went. The farmer's wife was told never to allow the old witch into the house again, nor to have any dealing with her. It was of course though too late, and a transaction had been made with a black witch. As we have come to expect, the farm began losing its livestock to mysterious deaths; however this farmer sought the help of a white witch immediately and without hesitation. We are not told what methods were employed to lift the ill-influence from the farm in this case; however, we do know that the farmer was told that the one who had injured him would be 'marked out' for all to see. Shortly after, the old witch woman's eye began to waste away in its socket, the sight of which became so hideous that she was compelled to wear a patch to hide it. Word having spread of the farmer's consultation with the white witch, it was confirmed to all in the area that the old woman was an evil doer, causing her to be utterly ostracized and abhorred by all.

The woman had a beautiful daughter who was at the time engaged, however, as a result of the foregoing events her intended broke off the engagement, spurning his love; for he would not marry the daughter of a witch. Following his rejection of the witch's daughter, he was severely injured at work; leaving him a cripple for life. The witch's daughter was around the same time struck down with a strange illness, and quickly wasted away. Before she died she was heard to say that her mother had 'drawn the circle' for her love, but that she had walked into it instead.

Within the instructions given to this family by the 'white witches' they consulted, we find again the familiar removal of the hearts from animals, dead of bewitchment, to be burnt or buried. As in the story of the beggar witch, we have seen also one of the magical methods of the West Country 'black witch', that of 'drawing the circle'. This had the potential to be a rather risky and foolhardy operation of bewitchment; for it involved drawing a circle upon the ground that would cause the death of the next living thing to enter it. There are numerous accounts of West Country witches 'drawing the circle' upon a pathway they knew their intended victim would soon walk along, and as such it was a means of killing by stealth. However, it did of course carry the enormous risk that someone other than the intended victim will pass along the spot first and take the fatal influence. Some witches, like the beggar witch, were more audacious, and ensured the success of the operation by drawing the death circle directly around their victim.

Another case involving the use of animal hearts was reported in *The Western Times* on the 27th of October, 1860. A Farmer from the Drewsteignton area lost two of his horses when they suddenly died. Although both horses were apparently fairly elderly, their deaths were quickly attributed to witchcraft.

Two renowned white witches; 'Tuckett' and 'Thomas', who would normally be consulted on such matters, had both passed away, but the farmer was advised by his neighbours that there was one such practitioner left at Crediton. Immediately, he saddled his nag and set out to the dwelling of the white witch 'Professor S'. Here, during the consultation, the 'old incantations were put in practice' and the farmer was shown, presumably by some method of scrying, 'the features of his bewitching enemy'. He was advised also of a ritual procedure to be carried out to break any further influence of the 'black witch'. The cost of the consultation is recorded as having been twenty-five shillings.

Upon his return, the farmer set about following the white witch's instructions by exhuming the dead bodies of his bewitched horses, in order to remove the hearts of each animal. These he stuck all over with pins and blackthorns, and wrapped them in brown paper. A great amount of green ashen wood and one cwt. of coal was built into a fire which, as night fell, was lit, and both hearts were consigned to the tremendous flames.

The use of Ash wood to build the ritual fire for spell-breaking purposes is again interesting; for it will be remembered that in the story of 'The Black Witch's Imp', a bowl of ash wood was employed in which to burn some of the blood of one of the farmer's bewitched animals.

By Salt & Silence 🍂

During consultations with a white witch, where ill-wishing is suspected, it is often mentioned that the practitioner divines the identity of the culprit. However, it was also often the case that the client was aided or directed in carrying out the divination for themselves; a risky business which could have serious consequences, and some stories from Devonshire reveal some of the methods used.

In one case, from the area of Stoke Gabriel, a farmer found his pigs were mysteriously dying. The farmer's wife travelled to Exeter in order to consult with a famous white witch. He advised her that the cause of their problem was, as suspected, black witchcraft, and that the ill-influence would be lifted by scattering a circle of salt around the house.

To discover the identity of the black witch, the couple should rise early the next morning, and remain silent and seated until a particular time in the afternoon. Then, the farmer's wife was to get up and leave the house. The first person she would meet upon doing so would be the black witch who had placed their evil influence upon their pigs.

The white witch's instructions were followed faithfully, however, upon leaving the house, the first person to be met by the farmer's wife was the kind and gentle wife of the neighbouring farmer. As the couple had always been on the friendliest of terms with her, the silent vigil must surely have failed. However, so great was their faith in the white witch's instructions that they accused and bullied the poor old lady, thus sadly ending what was before a valued friendship.

Silence was again a vital ingredient in a Devonshire case reported in *The Gloucester Citizen* on the 19th of August, 1879. In the North Devon parish of Charles, a farmer travelled to Exeter to consult with a white witch, as he believed he had been bewitched by a relative. The white witch returned with the farmer to his home in order to perform her rites of counter-witchery.

She instructed the farmer and his wife that strict silence should be observed throughout the procedure, which involved the burning of 'some compound resembling incense' and the repeating of an incantation. The farmer's wife however lacked the ability to keep silence, and made 'some contemptuous observations'. Perhaps this interruption ruined the white witch's ritual, for instead she prescribed that the farmer should live on a diet of beef for one week, during which time he was not to leave his home.

By Scrying Water ✄

A contemporary account in the 1908 *Devonshire Characters and Strange Events*, tells of a cattle-dealer who consulted with a white witch because his daughter had suffered influenza and remained 'rather strange in her head'. The witch showed the worried father a glass of water, and directed him to gaze into it to see the culprit who had overlooked his daughter, saying that whoever it was had fair hair and was of a stout body. Also the witch told the man that this person had never been inside his doors, but would enter them on the following Saturday.

The anxious father peered into the glass of water, and on its dancing surface he fancied he saw the reflection of a woman who lived not far from him. He returned to his home full of anger for the woman he was now convinced had bewitched his daughter.

The following night, a strange crackling sound awoke the husband of the suspected ill-wisher, and going out of the cottage to investigate he found the thatch ablaze. He rushed back inside to awaken his family, and all managed to escape, just as the roof fell in consuming the entire cottage in flame.

Upon investigating, the police found evidence that the fire had been started deliberately, as a stamp, which had fallen out of someone's pocket, and a number of spent matches were discovered on the ground by a hedge. It seemed that someone had climbed upon it to set the thatch alight.

The Wrong Chemise ✎

Whilst divinations to uncover a suspected ill-wisher could result in such near-fatal events, others had more amusing consequences. In a village outside Exeter lived a farm labourer who came down with a sudden illness. In search of a cure, he went to see the Exeter white witch, who revealed to him that the cause of his malady was his neighbour who had cast the evil eye upon him. To lift the black witch's curse, the man was instructed to obtain an article of his neighbour's clothing. This was to be rolled around a stone and secured with string. Before the moon rose the following night, the bundle was to be taken to the village pond and thrown into its centre.

The next day, the farm labourer made his way to the village inn to wait, and have a few courage building drinkies, until the time came when the moon would soon be rising. When he felt the time was right, the man left the pub and went nervously and quietly into his neighbour's garden in search of clothes; as he knew on that day there would be some hanging out on the line. Fumbling about in the dark, he snatched the first article he touched, wrapped it about a stone and tied it with string before making a hasty escape from the scene.

Finally, he reached the village pond, anxious not to be observed, and threw the item right into the middle, before returning home; relieved that the task had been done and could be forgotten about. The next morning however, the labourer's wife was furious; shrieking and ranting that her best chemise had been stolen – as it turns out, the farmer had partaken of a little too much 'Dutch courage' in the village inn the night before and, in his intoxicated state, had stumbled into his own garden by mistake.

Some Devonshire Witch Bottles ❧

In addition to the stories and accounts of people employing various means to combat the influence of the black witch, insights are given also where physical artefacts of such practices are left behind. A common physical survival of traditional counter-magic is the witch bottle, and in Devonshire, a good number of notable examples have turned up, including the following.[3]

During the preparation of a grave, close to the door of St George's Church in Monkleigh, North Devon, a witch bottle was discovered by the sexton. The green glass bottle was sealed with a cork which had been stuck with as many pins as it was possible to insert. The sexton had been instructed to rebury any items he might uncover during the digging of graves in the yard, and so the bottle was reburied; and thus probably remains there to this day.

In 1970, when a fifteenth century cottage in Chagford was undergoing renovations, a bottle was found concealed beneath the floor. Again, the bottle was of green glass and had been buried neck downwards. The bottle was opened in order to examine its contents, resulting in a foul smelling liquid bursting out. As well as the fluid, the bottle was found to contain a number of hand made pins and seventeen blackthorn spikes in a perfect state of preservation. A folklore expert at Exeter University was consulted who concluded that the liquid was, of course, most likely to be human urine.

Another witch bottle was found by workmen in a Bradworthy cottage, also buried beneath the floor, but this time made of earthenware. Upon examination the bottle was found to contain a number of pins, and what seemed to be 'decomposed flesh'. Also in Bradworthy, another witch bottle was discovered where two paths crossed in the churchyard of St. John the Baptist Church.

---

3. Farquharson-Coe, A. *Devon's Witchcraft*, p.5.

The find was taken by the curate to a local inn to see what others would make of it. Upon sight of the artefact, the inn's landlady fled in horror, and none of the villagers, who seemed quite fearful of the object, would admit to any knowledge of what it was and wished not to talk about it at all.

Housed in the collection of the Museum of Witchcraft & Magic, there are two interesting examples of Devonshire witch bottles. One is a bellarmine type; perhaps the most iconic and recognisable vessel used in traditional bottle magic. As most examples are, this bottle was found concealed within the fabric of a building; in this case within a wall in a house in the Sutton Harbour area of Plymouth. Its discovery came about after the house was bombed during the war. This example is particularly interesting because, whilst the use of bellarmine jars in magic is associated with the 17th and 18th centuries, the content of this one date its use and concealment from the late 19th to the early 20th century. So, we appear to have here an example of an old magical tradition in use in relatively recent times.[4]

Another witch bottle in the collection, also discovered during bomb damage clearance in Plymouth, was found to contain bone splinters which had been painted, along with hair and small pins; all within what was probably the decayed remains of urine.[5]

The Case of the Cursed Tin 🥀

This bizarre story concerns a family who lived not far from Crediton. One day, a man who enjoyed busying himself with woodwork was most grateful when a neighbour of his presented him with a tin full of a large amount of assorted nails. Strangely, the neighbour left the area very shortly afterwards and was not heard of

---

4. The Museum of Witchcraft & Magic, object no.14.

5. *Ibid*, object no.222.

again. The woodworker made good use of the handy collection of nails, however, when the time came that the last nail had been used, the empty tin revealed itself to be bewitched. No matter where the tin was kept; in cupboard, box or drawer, nor how securely, the tin would escape; bursting forth and hitting the ceiling before rolling wildly about the floor.

A white witch was consulted and a set of instructions were given by him. The bewitched tin was to be taken at midnight upon a moonless night to a deep pool, and there the tin must be thrown right into the pool's middle. These instructions the woodworker carried out faithfully, and as the tin hit the dark water's surface, it issued forth a loud hissing sound before sinking instantly as though it were a heavy rock, and not the empty sealed item it was that, by nature, should have floated.

SKIN-TURNING & FAMILIAR SPIRITS

One recurring characteristic of the traditional British magical practitioner, whether they be labelled 'black witch', 'white witch', 'conjurer', 'cunning man' or 'wise woman' etc. is the presence of a familiar spirit; who it seems was a primary source of the practitioner's occult power and magical knowledge. The Devonshire practitioner was no different.

Another characteristic is the ability of the practitioner to transform into the likeness of some animal, and again this was a power possessed equally by the 'black' and 'white' witch alike.

Some accounts and stories from Devonshire involving magical animals are clear cases of 'skin-turning', such as those telling of 'witch-hares'; where a witch has been seen to have the ability to go forth in the likeness of a hare. Such an ability is often only revealed when a wounded hare has been followed by a huntsman, leading to the discovery of an elderly woman exhibiting an injury on her body; corresponding to that which had been inflicted upon the hare.

There are numerous stories of this kind from Devonshire; such as that of 'Old Moll' of Chagford, given earlier in this book. Another, from the early 19th century, tells of the case of Molly Bryant of Bideford. She was an elderly woman, living in an almshouse, and was reputed locally to be a witch and to possess the ability to transform herself into the likeness of a hare. She would enjoy doing this specifically to annoy the local huntsman; by leading them on a long and fruitless chase.

One man, a soldier, took it upon himself to take revenge upon the witch-hare. He sat, covertly watching Molly Bryant's home, until he saw the witch-hare 'spying' through the keyhole. He took aim and fired at the creature, whereupon it immediately disappeared.

A search was made of the old woman's home, and she was found with an injury to her leg. From that day until her death, the locals firmly believed that she had been shot by the soldier whilst in the act of jumping through her keyhole in the form of a hare.[6]

Whilst the hare seems to have been a favorite form taken by shape-shifting witches in Devonshire, there are also accounts of witches taking on the form of the fox. One such witch was said to have transformed into the likeness of a fox in order to take chickens from the local farms. One night however, whilst the witch-fox was raiding farm's henhouse, the farmer was awoken by the noise and rushed to the scene with his shotgun. Upon seeing the fox he took fire; hitting and wounding the animal.

Of course, just as in the stories of witch-hares, a reclusive, elderly woman had been found in the village the next day; suffering with gunshot wounds. She was taken to hospital but soon died of her injuries.[7]

In other stories, the nature of the animal involved is not quite so clear to us. The distinction between the witch and her familiar is sometimes blurred, and we are left wondering if the magical creature is the witch herself in bestial disguise, or a spirit sent forth to carry out her will, or to impart her magical influence upon her target. As we have seen in the use of 'witch bottles' and suchlike, there is a mysterious link between a witch and the results of her magic; a link which could be exploited

6. Gent, Frank. *The Trial of the Bideford Witches*, p.22.

7. Howard, Michael. *West Country Witches*, p.125-126.

by the witch's victim as a 'return path' for the working of retaliative counter-magic.

Sometimes the retaliation against a witch need not be consciously magical in nature; indeed the victim need not be aware that witchcraft had been behind the appearance of a nuisance-causing creature at all. The discovery that witchcraft had been the cause was sometimes only made when an elderly woman was found dead or wounded, and exhibiting the same injuries as those that had been inflicted upon the creature, usually a toad, just as in the cases of 'witch hares', but this time the body of the toad is still where it had been left.

Such circumstances reveal both the corporeal and magical nature of a familiar; having inhabited a physical bestial body, but being magically linked to the witch herself; as though the familiar spirit is part of the witch; being a vehicle and vessel of her magical will.

One account of a Devonshire witch and her mysterious link with a toad familiar, which is supposed to be true, was related by Robert Hunt in his *Popular Romances of the West of England*. An elderly woman, known as Aunt Alsey, was the tenant of a small cottage in Anthony, belonging to a Devonport shopkeeper. She possessed such an unpleasant character and violent temper that it earned for her the reputation of being a witch.

Aunt Alsey had become seriously behind with her rent, but each time her landlord, a rather quiet and kind-hearted man, called by for his money she gave him nothing but abuse. One day, the shopkeeper walked to Anthony, determined to have his rent and turn the old woman out of his cottage. Aunt Alsey, as usual, turned violent and vicious, but this time sat herself in the doorway to the cottage and cursed her landlord's wife, his child that she was carrying, and all that belonged to him. The poor man fled in terror to his home. Enquiring of her husband whether he had any success with the old woman, he told her of what had occurred. She told him to rest from his ordeal and went to tend the shop and serve a customer who had just come in.

Upon weighing one of the items for the customer, something fell from the ceiling; striking the beam of the shop scales right out of her hand. Both women screamed at the sight of a large toad, sprawling on the shop counter amidst the tangled chains of the scales. The shopkeeper, still nervous from his encounter with Aunt Alsey, rushed into the shop to see what all the commotion was about, seized the toad with the fire tongs, and threw the poor creature behind a log burning in the hearth. His wife, normally a woman of strong nerves, fainted, and although soon restored to her senses, the fainting fits returned again and again. Concerned for the safety of his wife and unborn child, the man sent urgently for the doctor.

While they were attending to his wife, the shopkeeper's young daughter, who when grown was Hunt's informant, let out cries of terror from the parlor; 'O father, the toad, the toad!' He rushed downstairs to find the poor creature had escaped death, although badly burnt, and was now trying to escape over the fender. He took up the tongs again, this time with the intention of removing the toad from the house, but before he could act, a man from Anthony ran in the shop to inform him that a doctor had been sent for Aunt Alsey, as she had fallen into her fire and was badly burnt, as was much of the cottage which had caught light from the old woman's burning dress.

With no chance of survival for one so old and so severely injured, Aunt Alsey was carried to the workhouse, where every effort was made to make her as comfortable as possible, although she never regained consciousness and died in the night.

While the shopkeeper was on his way to Anthony, his servant had taken up the tongs to remove the toad, throwing it with a shudder on a flowerbed behind the house. The next morning it was found dead, and when examined by the shopkeeper the toad was found to have injuries corresponding exactly to those suffered by the old woman; further securing the belief for all that old Aunt Alsey had indeed been a witch.

Another story is told of two neighboring ladies from the Kingsbridge area of South Devon.[8] The two were friends and were in the habit of taking a daily walk together. As they began one of their excursions, a harsh storm erupted; forcing the two ladies to return to their homes to wait for the storm to pass.

One of the women decided to make some pancakes; something for which she was particularly noted, however on this occasion she was unable to produce anything; the batter refusing to set despite her best efforts. During her struggle; in which she was becoming increasingly infuriated, she suddenly noticed a large toad sitting right at the back of the fire, watching her labours. As toads in Devonshire had long been believed to be witches in disguise, or their familiar spirits, the woman took it that the toad was the cause of her difficulty and had set an ill-influence upon her efforts. In a rage she flung the contents of her frying pan at the creature which instantly and mysteriously vanished into thin air. Regaining her composure, a fresh mixture was prepared and perfect pancakes made without difficulty or hindrance.

When the storm had finally passed, the woman went to call on her neighbour to ask if she would like to reattempt their walk. Her neighbour's daughter, however, came to the door in a distressed state explaining that her mother had suddenly experienced a bad injury. The woman made her way to her neighbour's bedchamber to find her in bed with her face terribly scalded. Concluding that the toad was in fact her neighbour in disguise, the injured woman was marked in the community as a black witch for life.

---

8. Farquharson-Coe, A. *Devon's Witchcraft*, p.10-11.

Within West Country witch-lore, the toad has a most persistent and recurring presence. As we have seen in this chapter, and earlier in this book, the toad might be the witch in batrachian form, a familiar spirit, or a companion and aid in the crafting of magic. Like the 'toad witch' of North Bovey, numerous examples exist of those known or suspected to be magical practitioners, keeping toads, sometimes in large quantities; cosseting them in earthenware vessels or letting them walk freely about the cottage.[9]

We shall encounter the toad again later in this book within the collection of operative Devonshire charms and examples of folk-magic, with which the toad has a long history and association of mixed fortunes. Other than the often decidedly cruel uses to which toads were put in popular magic and cure-charms, how were toads employed magically by the Devonshire toad-witches themselves, who kept and cosseted these lovable creatures? Whilst we will never know the secrets of how the North Bovey witch would operate at midnight in the churchyard with her toads, insights into Devonshire toad-witcherie are given by Michael Howard.[10]

In 1900 there lived a toad-witch in Bishops Teignton, who employed toads to place curses upon enemies. This was achieved by placing a toad on the doorstep of the victim, and when they opened the door, they would catch the gaze of the toad by which the ill-influence would be imparted, and illness would immediately strike.

Another toad-witch of North Devon in the 1930s would also employ toads in curse magic. She would make incantations over her toads and then she would gently touch them on the head whilst ill-wishing her victims. It seems she must have had some success, as others would visit and pay money to the witch to have curses placed on their enemies via this method.

---

9. Howard, Michael. *West Country Witches*, p.115.
10. *Ibid*, p.116.

The Devonshire cunning man, Cecil Williamson, wrote beautifully of the special relationship existing between the witch and the toad;

'Dear, dear friendly old toad. If you have never kept one or been on friendly terms with one in your garden, then you have missed out on one of the joys of the good Lord's creations. For under their ugly rough exterior there beats a heart full of affection for anyone who cares to treat and talk to them with love and respect. The witches discovered this fact of nature centuries ago. What is more, showing kindness to ugly and repellent human beings and animals brings rich rewards to the givers of affection. Example the befriended ugly old woman in Cinderella, picking up sticks in the forest - who turns out to be the fairy queen with magical powers of benefaction, and so on in a thousand tales of legends gathered from around the world. Little wonder that the witches of Devon and Cornwall cosseted, pampered and befriended these strange loveable magical creatures who have the fairy power to bring rich rewards. So be warned - be kind to toads.' [11]

The familiar, whether manifest in the form of some corporeal creature, or present purely as a liminal spirit entity, is closely associated and bound with the body and being of the witch.

Despite the pervasive presence of the familiar spirit in British witch tradition, it is an aspect notable by its strange absence in Gerald Gardner's vision for the Craft, and as a consequence the popular modern Craft movement as a whole. Cecil Williamson, knowing of the prevalence for working with the spirit world amongst the 'wayside witches' found this an odd situation;

'I tried to get Gerald Gardner interested in this idea of the familiar spirit. And, similarly, today it is very hard to find a vicar that you can go to and have a reasonably sensible conversation about angels and yet you walk through their churches and see them all over.' [12]

---

11. Museum of Witchcraft & Magic, object no.205.

12. 'A Conversation with Cecil Williamson', *Talking Stick* No.7.

Much of Cecil's writing, some of which was written to accompany the artefacts and forms of magic exhibited in his museum, tell of the central importance of the familiar spirit to the operations of the witches, wise women, and wayside practitioners he encountered and spoke with in his investigations. The 'old-time' witch, Cecil explains, believed that everything possessed a 'spirit force', and upon this they would call for help when in need. Most important however was the belief in a personal spirit – the familiar spirit. Cecil explained that the familiar spirit was a kind of 'guardian angel' or a spirit guide; there to watch over, give counsel, advice and companionship to the witch. Those who cultivated relationships with a personal familiar spirit, he tells us, gained *'peace of mind and an unasked for power to help other people in stressful situations.'* [13]

Cecil also shares with us as insights into the ways in which the magical practitioner might attract and house a helpful spirit with which to establish a working relationship. Some such 'spirit houses' featured in his collection are in the form of skulls; and the human skull appears to have been a particularly prized accoutrement of the traditional spirit working witch. There are of course a number of skulls, both human and animal, resident within the Museum of Witchcraft & Magic today; each with their own story telling of different ways in which skulls may be employed within the work of the witch. Each one also illustrates vividly the vital importance of spirits and the spirit world within the old ways of witchcraft. In one of his old museum description cards, Cecil Williamson explains this importance;

The human skull is the symbol of death. For the witch death holds a strange fascination. Each and every one of us is born to die, but is death a final end to life? The witch says no. For she knows that: "there are other places and other things". Her whole

---

13. Williamson, Cecil. *Whatever Happened to the Old Time Witches?*

life and being is devoted to the ever present but unseen world of spirit. To the witch the spirit world is a reality, a living thing. To her everything has a spirit, a soul, a personality, be it animal, mineral, vegetable. That is why to us in the south west we know and believe in the little people, oh, you may laugh, my fine up country folk, but beware for indeed you are in the land where ghoulies and ghosties, and long legged beasties still romp, stomp and go bump in the night. Come, let us show you what the witches and their spirits do.'

One skull from the Museum's collection, with its cut calvaria, was employed as a 'wish box' by a witch from the Heavitree area of Exeter, and is dated 1920. A wish box is a closable container used magically by placing within it a written request, or an item symbolic of that which is desired. The act of placing and enclosing a magical request within a specially prepared container, where we can no longer see it, we might see as symbolic of putting our request to the Otherworld and leaving it in the hands of the spirits, or in this particular case to 'Old Nick'; the personification of magical power, the unknown and 'otherness'.

It is an often repeated piece of magical advice that a spell, once performed, should be forgotten about or at least not dwelt upon. The symbolic use of a wish box; to hold your desire unseen, to be left and walked away from, could aid this process; allowing the magic to 'get on with it' unhindered. What better form of wish box to make your requests to the spirit world than a lidded skull?

A spirit, resident in a skull, might also serve a witch as an oracle and a spirit world advisor, as is shown in another human skull resident in the museum; particularly striking because of its red painted iron holder in the form of a five pointed star. We are told it belonged to a witch called 'Old Granny Mann' who lived in the North Bovey area of Devon. She referred to this skull, or perhaps the spirit that it housed, as her friend, and kept it in a secret spot on Easdon Tor. To this remote place she would sometimes go when presented with a question or a difficult problem by a client, in order to consult her spirit friend for advice. One could imagine that the spirit occupied skull, and the remote and numinous location of Easdon Tor would combine to create an ideal circumstance for contact and communication with the world of spirit. The act of walking can also be a meditative or a contemplative one, and so the witch's journey to and from the secret spot might also aid the finding of a solution.

Other bones, human and animal, have also been employed by the Devonian witch to house spirits and spirit-force. The use of bone for such purposes within magic is quite understandable; for it is a substance accustomed to housing, supporting, and making mobile a spirit in life, und thus, as an empty vessel in death, it is for the magician an ideal item within which to call forth the presence of spirits.

Amongst the spirit-filled items collected from south west witches by Cecil Williamson, we also find snake bones. The snake is of great magical significance to some present day witches; being the ancient symbol of the telluric fire – the spirit potency in the land. Within the museum collection there are two beautiful witch necklaces made using snake vertebrae. One example, strung with red and blue beads, is from the Collumpton area. Its description card tells us that the red beads symbolise blood and the blue symbolise air, and that these necklaces *'confer upon the witch a degree of magical and spiritual power.'* [14]

As well as skulls and bones, other vessels have been put to use by the south west witch. In the Museum of Witchcraft and Magic we also encounter the tradition of the witch's spirit house in the form of spirit jars; which

---

14. Museum of Witchcraft & Magic, description card for object no.366.

may be part filled with all manner of materials and items to keep the spirit happy, comfortable and entertained. An example from Devonshire's neighbor, Somerset, is filled with a bottom layer of tiny black pebbles, then white pebbles upon which rest a puff ball, an open egg shell, sycamore seeds, a lily root and bulb, a lump of sulphur and a bra. Cecil writes enigmatically of this spirit jar; '*The thinking behind such fabrications is complicated to say the least, and calls for a deal of folklore knowledge and an understanding of the world of spirit force. My advice, leave well alone. Just smile and say "all rather quaint, isn't it?" And then move on.*'

The Devonshire witch, Levannah Morgan, writes of her approach to the 'Devon Spirit Jar' in her delightful, and immensely practical book '*A Witch's Mirror*';

'*To make your empty jar into a spirit jar, you are going to put things into it that spirits like. When I first did this I worked with the things that Cecil Williamson taught me about but over the years I have let the spirits guide me and used the things they have told me they want. Traditional Devon items to put in a spirit jar include small quartz pebbles, little seashells (cowries and pink "fairy toenails" are good), feathers, bits of mirror and glass worn smooth by the sea, ears of barley or wheat and a piece of red wool or thread with nine knots in it.*'

A particularly pretty example of a south west witch's spirit house in the museum's collection is formed from an old lace maker's globe, which would once have been filled with water to act as a magnifier. It has been filled instead with pink and white 'hundreds and thousands' and a spirit invited into it by a Honiton-based witch named Katie Day. Despite the sweet appearance, it was said that the spirit housed within this set up 'could be quite nasty at times.'

As we have seen in Devonshire witch-lore, the witch and the familiar spirit are intimately bound, and this tradition is reflected in the writings of Cecil Williamson where we find that, amongst the various items employed, the spirit house par excellence is the witch's own body:

'As every woman knows, you can regard your body as a structure in which a living force can grow. This is so easy for a woman as, after all, they carry a child for quite a length of time. If you have a mental picture of your body being a temple, or B&B if you like, and you want a familiar spirit, this is what you have to do. You do not want to have the place like a rat's nest. You have to be very good and really rather dull.' [15]

Being 'very good', and 'rather dull' would seem to tell of a simpler approach to the old traditions and practices of self-sacrifice and purification; undertaken by those magicians seeking attainment of the familiar spirit, and found in complex form within the old grimoires. Cecil was himself a teetotaller, which is likely to have been an aspect of his own occult devotional purification and abstinence for the maintenance of a relationship with his familiar spirit.

Cecil reveals other prerequisites to attracting the familiar spirit to the *'temple of the body'*, for he tells us it is necessary to develop *'a fuel force'*, which is obtained by devoting one's self to *'a life of love and goodness towards all living things which have within them the pulse of life'*.[16] People cultivating such spirit relationships would, of course, not be understood by the 'ordinary folk' and could be viewed as highly suspect, even if useful, and so as Cecil explained; *'those who follow the path of the All-seeing Eye keep a low profile and live, so to speak, in a world within a world and keep to themselves'*.[17]

For the ceremonial magicians, knowledge of, and conversation with the familiar spirit was an equally vital and striven for magical accomplishment; of course attained via far more complex and elaborate rites than

---

15. 'A Conversation with Cecil Williamson', *Talking Stick* No.7.

16. Williamson, Cecil. *Whatever Happened to the Old Time Witches?*

17. *Ibid.*

those employed by the old-time west country witch. Both approaches however share a central theme of self-sacrifice, self-purification and immense devotion.

Some of Cecil Williamson's writings tell of rites and ways for attaining the familiar spirit which, although simple in their approach, are no less physically, mentally and spiritually demanding.

For example, he describes '*The Ritual of the Ordeal*' which requires the witch to venture out to some lonely out building. There, on the cold floor, the witch will lay herself down with her limbs outstretched, and remain motionless in that position, in the dark, for hours or even days at a time; however long is necessary for the desired result to be achieved. The desired result is to acquire '*spirit force*' and union with the world of spirit.

Eventually, the spirit will separate from the body and in that moment the reality of the spirit world is revealed unto the witch, and it is in this immersion into the realms of spirit that the union takes place for the 'spirit force' becomes one with the witch; entering and taking 'possession of her through the gateway of her soul'.[18] This union with the familiar spirit is likened by Cecil Williamson to sexual union with the Succubus. To engage in such an encounter, he says, is '*to drink from the cup of forbidden knowledge.*' [19]

A similar rite is hinted at in a description label; beautifully written by Cecil to accompany an intriguing painting in the Museum of Witchcraft and Magic's collection. It depicts a naked woman lying in the branches of a tree in the depths of a dark wood. All about her, spirit eyes peer out from the night. The label reads:

'*If you go down into the woods tonight you will be in for a big surprise. Naked, alone, high up in a tree deep in the heart of a*

18. Patterson, Steve. *Cecil Williamson's Book of Witchcraft*, p.246.
19. *Ibid.*

wood at dark of night is quite something. For a start you have left mankind and its brash world behind. Now you are a stranger in the world of nature, the green growing world, where fear is the trigger that releases the spirit force. Like a snail without its shell you are at the mercy of the smallest gnat and then it happens. The spirit cloak of protection descends and enfolds one and you can feel the warmth and well being of the other world. Then it is that you become aware that there are indeed other places and other things. Some describe it as feeling the finger of god upon them, peace, perfect peace. The spirit eyes keep watch over you, you are utterly safe.'

A far more elaborate ritual setting, for what seems to have been much the same purpose, was depicted in a museum tableau of Cecil's titled '*The Ordeal of the Witches' Cradle*'.[20] A wrought iron frame was hung from a ceiling beam by a chain, and beneath it was set a large incense burner. The witch would lie, constrained, upon the frame; swinging gently to and fro above the rising incense fumes until an altered state of consciousness is achieved. It is in this state that '*complete union with the spirit world*' will be experienced.

Within these rites we find lengthy devotional acts, fear, discomfort, and altered states of consciousness employed as catalysts for attaining union with the spirit world, or the familiar spirit. Perhaps in these acts is the suggestion that the familiar spirit is not something entirely separate from oneself; to be sought and captured, but rather that it is an aspect of oneself, and via such rites, the witch seeks to perceive and gain knowledge of this aspect of her being.

Certainly, Cecil Williamson himself was known to identify his familiar spirit with his own shadow, and would converse and consult with his shadow for advice and guidance on important matters.[21]

---

20. Patterson, Steve. *Cecil Williamson's Book of Witchcraft*, p.247.
21. *Ibid.* p.243.

In a recorded interview, held in the Museum of Witchcraft & Magic archives, Cecil imparts two pieces of advice for those who would seek to follow the way of the witch; first, contact your shadow, and second, live a good life!

WITCHES & *the* LAW

itches and magical practitioners have always been in a rather precarious business; running the risk of coming to the negative attentions of the Church, legal authorities, and their own neighbours.

In law, the working of magic, for beneficial purposes or for harm, has in Britain fluctuated from mortally illegal to being regarded as merely a problematic and disruptive social pheno menon.

As belief in the efficacy of witchcraft, magic, and the 'occult sciences' waned amongst the authorities and social elite, so the laws regarding such things were modified and re-worked through successive 'Witchcraft Acts'; beginning in 1542 with a Bill against *'conjuraracons & wichecraftes and sorcery and enchantmants.'* These terms covered the uses of divination to tell where *'thinges lost or stollen shulde be become'*, making invocations and dealing with spirits. By this act of parliament, any who were convicted of these acts *'shall have and suffre such paynes of deathe losse and forfaytures of their lands tentes goodes and Catalles'*.

By 1736, the Witchcraft Act of that year established the activities of those who practised 'witchcraft, sorcery inchantment, or conjuration' as acts of fraud; no longer punishable by death, but instead by a maximum sentence of one year in prison without bail.[22]

With the ever-onward advancement of industrial development and scientific thinking ruling the day, dealing

---

22. Davies, Owen. *Popular Magic*, p.20-21.

with such matters as 'witchcraft' became something of an embarrassment to 19th century legal authorities. And so, with the 1824 Vagrancy Act being passed by parliament, this became the law by which those who told fortunes, worked charms, or consulted with spirits, would most often be charged; despite those accused sometimes being relatively well-to-do home owners, and not 'vagrants' by any stretch of the imagination.[23]

However, even long before the acts of 1824 and 1736, the judiciary sometimes showed reluctance to give credence to the belief in witchcraft and magic, and turned to fraud instead as the basis for prosecution. In Devonshire for example, in 1636, Margaret Snelling was prosecuted for deceiving and deluding by fortune telling. She was punished by being whipped, pilloried, and ordered to do penance on four consecutive Sundays in three different churches.[24]

In another 17th century Devonshire case, the reality of the witchcraft for which the accused had been brought before the law was again rejected. In 1696, Elizabeth Horner was accused by William Bovet in Exeter of bewitching three of his children. One child had died and another suffered a deformity of the legs; causing her to go about on her hands and knees.

It was claimed that Elizabeth would, by witchcraft, cause the children to be bitten, pricked and pinched, with the resulting marks upon their bodies still visible as evidence.

More fantastical 'evidence' against her, given in court, included stories that the children had brought up crooked pins, that the deformed child would suddenly leap five feet into the air, and another of the children did five or six times walk nine feet up a smooth plaster wall; laughing as she did so and saying that Bess Horner was holding her up.

---

23. Davies, Owen. *Popular Magic*, p.24.

24. *Ibid*, p.10.

The children also swore that Elizabeth Horner's head would detach from her shoulders and walk on its own quietly into their stomachs.

On Elizabeth's shoulder, there was said to be some kind of wart, which the children said was her 'witch-mark' and which she used to suckle her imp; a toad.

The Lord Chief Justice Holt 'shook his head' and declared Elizabeth Horner not guilty. He is said to have given the same verdict to every other case of supposed witchcraft brought before him.[25]

A case was reported in 1869 of the mothers of 'two or three young women' from Dittisham in South Devon, who went to Teignmouth to consult with a 'wizard' because they suspected ill-wishing to be the cause of their daughters having fallen ill.

The Teignmouth wizard confirmed that the girls were indeed 'deeply wounded' (by witchcraft) but promised that he would be able to cure them. A 'good round sum' was paid to him by the women, however their daughters remained unwell and the wizard declared the girls to be beyond help.

Undeterred however, the women consulted instead with a 'witch' who lived in Dartmouth. 'Many pounds' were paid to her, and it appeared that the witch's spells worked; for the girls quickly recovered from their mysterious illness. Following this success, the witch demanded a final payment of £4, however the women were unable to raise any further money. They decided instead to arrange for a friend to visit the Dartmouth witch and threaten to take her before the magistrates if she persisted in demanding her payment. So alarmed was she by this threat, that she not only waved her claim to the £4, but also returned part of the money she had already been paid.[26]

---

25. Linton, E. Lynn. *Witch Stories.*

26. *The Luton Times and Advertiser*, February 27th 1869.

Even if a practitioner's magic was apparently successful, demanding large sums in payment from the client was evidently risky, and we can assume both the 'witch' and the client would have been well aware that if such a matter were brought before the law, guilt of obtaining money by deception was assured. One has to wonder in this case however, why the women did not pursue a return of payment instead from the Teignmouth 'wizard' who's magic had apparently been so unsuccessful.

In 1892, the wife of a sick man consulted with a Devonshire 'cunning man' named Hilton. He made divinations using the traditional 'Bible and Key' method, and told the woman that she and her husband were under magical attack from a group of seven people; all of them he named. He supplied her with some herbal pills and a piece of rope 'with a mark on it', the latter he told her would provide magical protection for her husband. She first had to sew the piece of rope inside some black silk, and then conceal it within the lining of his coat.

Perhaps the charm and the pills failed to bring about a cure, for the woman took legal action against Hilton and he was charged in Ottery St Mary with obtaining a payment of twelve shillings by deception.[27]

'White witches' and 'cunning folk' faced other dangers from their own clients. Whether their work was successful or not, there was always great risk that the client could turn on the practitioner; accusing them of being a 'black witch' and the cause of their woes.

In the 15th century for example, a hereditary Devonshire 'wizard' named Michael Trevisard was consulted by a woman worried for her infant child, because her previous two children had both died. The wizard made a divination into the matter, and told the woman that, alas, the infant would not live long enough to run with other children.

---

27. Howard, Michael. *West Country Witches*, p.44.

Trevisard's prediction came true, for the child died soon after, with the result that he himself was accused of causing the death by bewitchment.[28]

In 1867, Mary Catherine Murray was brought before magistrates in Plymouth on charges of deception against her client, Thomas Rendle. Mary had a reputation for being able to help those who had been ill-wished, and so when Thomas's wife fell ill, which he believed to have been caused by witchcraft, he travelled to Plymouth to consult with her. Mary supplied Thomas Rendle with some powders and a charm inscribed on parchment and prescribed that his wife was to place the charm around her neck on the Sunday, and to burn the powders on the fire whilst reading aloud Psalm 91. She also supplied a bottle of medicine and for these things she charged £3. Mary also told him that his wife should gather prescribed herbs and plants from a churchyard for 21 consecutive nights, and for this advice she charged a guinea.[29]

During her trial, it became clear that Mary Murray did not consider her activities to be fraudulent, and genuinely believed in her own magical knowledge and abilities.[30]

The condition of Thomas Rendle's wife however did not improve, and, turning against Mary, he accused her of being the one who had bewitched her.

The parchment charm Mary had supplied was shown during the trial, along with a similar one which she herself had been wearing when she was arrested (suggesting that she did indeed have faith in her magical abilities). Details are given, although it is not certain which of the two charms these relate to specifically. Signs were inscribed on the parchment, along with the written words

---

28. Howard, Michael. *West Country Witches*, p.83.

29. *Ibid*, p.43.

30. *Ibid*.

'Whosoever beareth this sign all spirits do him homage... This sign is against witchcraft, putrid infection, and sudden death... Whosoever beareth this sign need fear no foe... and this is the sign against witchcraft and suicide, and against evil demons.' [31]

This appears to be a description of charms similar to those drawn from the two famous charms given in Reginald Scot's *The Discoverie of Witchcraft*; popularly used and supplied by 'cunning folk' to their clients.

Mary Catherine Murray was sentenced to three months' imprisonment with hard labour.

Witches, conjurers and the like did not always however appear in court as the accused. In the village of Ashburton on the edge of Dartmoor, for example, when books had been stolen from the village church, a local 'cunning woman' was consulted by the churchwarden. She divined that the thieves were two local men and gave their identities. When the men appeared in court accused of the theft, the cunning woman was called as a witness. When asked how she had discovered their identities, she said she had done it by 'shuffling the cards'.[32]

From the 19th century onwards, Devon's witches and magical practitioners, both actual and the merely

---

31. Lugger, Andrew. 'Magic Moments', article from *Solicitor's Journal*.

32. Howard, Michael. *West Country Witches*, p.52.

suspected, felt confident enough to make use of the courts for themselves when aggrieved. Such recourse was most often taken when a suspected witch had been attacked by those following the old tradition of 'scoring above the breath'; drawing blood from a witch to nullify his or her powers.

One such case occurred in 1815 in Plymouth. A baker and his wife had several children; all were strong, healthy and lively but one. This child was small and sickly and believed to have been 'wisht'; that is, under the influence of witchcraft. An elderly customer of the baker was blamed for the child having been 'overlooked', and the baker's wife, and her maid, set upon the elderly lady armed with long pins with which they made many cuts into her arms and neck. The elderly lady, having suffered such a violent attack, was lucky indeed not to have lost her life.

Public opinion was that the women acted correctly by drawing blood from the witch believed to be responsible. The judiciary however viewed it of course as an illegal and vicious act. The baker was ordered to pay £5 compensation for the savage attack made by his wife and maid.

Another case was reported in 1860 from the Petty Sessions of Woodbury, East Devon. An old woman named Susannah Sullock complained that she had been attacked by Virginia Hebden at Colpton Raleigh on the 8th of June. Susannah said; *'I was turning out my little cow in the brake, when I felt something touch me. I turned my head, and seeing the defendant, said "How you frightened me." She answered, "You want to be frightened for what you ha' done me." I said, "I have'nt a doo'd nothing to you," and she began to scratch me over my face and hands with something sharp. I was afraid she was going to kill me. She draw'd blood both on my face and hands'.*

Virginia Hebden was found guilty of attacking Susannah Sullock, and fined 14s. The newspaper report of the case ends; '*We noticed that witchcraft is very prevalent amongst the illiterate in the neighborough of Colyton, Salterton, and Woodbury*'.[33]

In 1881, a male 'white witch' had taken one of his clients, a farmer, before the Ottery St Mary magistrates after having been attacked and cut by him with a sharp instrument. During the case it was revealed that the farmer and his family had been suffering from illness, and that his father had gone to see the white witch for a cure. Black witchcraft was divined to be the cause of the family's illness, and the culprit; a particular neighbour of theirs.

Payment being given, the family were provided with pills and unpleasant substances to take. As no cure occurred, the farmer's father made another visit to the white witch who then told him that the witchcraft they were suffering from was stronger than he had previously thought, and therefore the cure would take longer and would require further payment. Produce from the farm, a silver watch, a pistol and £3 were handed over to the white witch.

However, rather than seeing any improvement, the family's illness worsened. Thus, the family began to suspect the white witch himself of prolonging and worsening their illness by magic in order to extract increasing payments.

Upon meeting the plaintiff, the accused farmer took hold of the white witch and cut at his hand before aiming also to attack him about the head. The farmer explained to the magistrates that he had been told that if he could draw the witch's blood, then the ill-influence would be lifted. After he had attacked the plaintiff, he claimed that the illness he had been suffering from had begun to leave him. The father, who had originally consulted the plaintiff, was asked if he also had been relieved of

33. *The Taunton Courier & Western Advertiser*, July18th 1860.

his illness following the attack his son had made. He replied that he had not, and believed that for his illness to be lifted, he would also have to draw blood from the plaintiff himself. The case was settled with the payment of a £1 fine.

The tradition was still known, believed in, and used in Devonshire as late as the mid-1920s; as reported in *The Western Daily Press*. A smallholder named Alfred John Matthews from Clyst St Lawrence, East Devon, was charged with assaulting his neighbour Ellen Garnsworthy. Ellen told the bench that Alfred had attacked her and caused her arm to bleed profusely by scratching it with a long pin, before threatening to shoot her.

Alfred Matthews admitted carrying out the attack, and said he had done so because Ellen had ill-wished both him and his pig. He appears to have believed that it was still illegal to be a witch, for he told the Magistrates that the police should raid her house where they would find, and should confiscate, a crystal that he claimed she possessed.

Although the Magistrates tried to convince him otherwise, he held firmly on to his belief in the reality and power of witchcraft. For the attack, he was sentenced to one month's imprisonment.[34]

Although practicing magic was not in itself illegal, it was not a legitimate trade afforded any legal rights or protection; as the Exeter 'cunning man' James Tuckett discovered in 1846 when he tried, unsuccessfully of course, to sue a client who had repossessed a horse given to him in payment for magical services.[35]

The Western Morning News reported an interesting case, which gave a little insight into the practices of a working witch in 1926. It also illustrates that the person concerned was regarded and identified as a 'witch' and

---

34. *The Western Daily Press*, December 9th 1924.

35. Davies, Owen. *Popular Magic*, p.25.

not a 'cunning woman', or any of the other names modern historians insist all professional rural magicians were instead known by.

In Kingsteignton, Matilda Anne Heard applied for divorce from her husband Samuel, on the grounds of his unreasonable behaviour. Samuel justified his behaviour by telling the court that his wife was a witch, and that she worked magic upon him; for example, while he slept in his chair, she had drawn a ring of salt on the floor around him. He also revealed that she operated a 'witchcraft business', and had observed her sticking pins into a bullock's heart (a traditional counter-cursing or protection charm), after which she had buried it in the garden. She would also perform divinations at the hearth by throwing chemicals into the fire, causing the flames to blaze vigorously so that she could stare into them for visions, and would plunge the fire tongs into the fire as a charm to keep evil spirits away.[36]

---

36. Howard, Michael. *West Country Witches*, p.71.

DADDY'S HOLE

THE DEVIL'S STONES

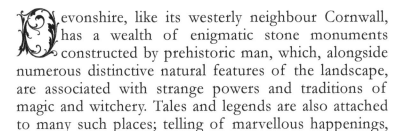

evonshire, like its westerly neighbour Cornwall, has a wealth of enigmatic stone monuments constructed by prehistoric man, which, alongside numerous distinctive natural features of the landscape, are associated with strange powers and traditions of magic and witchery. Tales and legends are also attached to many such places; telling of marvellous happenings, supernatural events, ghostly entities and the Devil himself.

An old name for the Devil in Devonshire is the *Dewer*, and this name is attached to a remarkable towering and jagged mass of rocky crags, rising out of a dense and eerie woodland of distorted trees. The Dewerstone, on the South West edge of Dartmoor, is heavily associated with the Devil; who in Devonshire folklore is often the leader of the Wild Hunt. It is here, at the Dewerstone, that the Wild Hunt in Devon is said to end up on each outing;

125

following its beginning from the hauntingly beautiful Wistman's Wood. This ghostly hunt is said to have been seen many times at Whetstone, and its terrified victims have been relentlessly perused by the Wild Hunt across the moor to the Summit of Dewerstone, whereupon the Hunt disappears, and the victim falls to their death; their soul to be claimed by 'Old Dewer ' himself.

For many years, this imposing rock face has been a popular destination for climbers; attracted by its challenging craggy ascent. There have however been numerous tragic accidents where climbers have fallen from the Dewerstone to their deaths; adding perhaps to the foreboding atmosphere of the place.

The association of the place with the Devil was doubtlessly made all the heavier one winter, when the face of the Dewerstone was covered with snow, within which could be seen a mysterious and impossible trail of hoof prints rising to its summit.[37]

Another Devonshire name for the Devil is 'Daddy', and in Torquay is another rock-face associated with both the Devil and the Wild Hunt. 'Daddy Hole' is a limestone cliff, rising seventy-five meters above the sea. In the mid-19th century, a story was collected in Torquay telling of a young maid who had fallen deeply in love; the object of her affections however was in love with another. Stricken with grief and heartache, the young maid would spend her evenings walking alone, along the cliff-tops, until on one of her lonely outings she heard the approach of the feared Wild Hunt. In terror she ran, but of course could not hope to escape, and fainted just as she was about to be run down by the crying hounds and the Devil's great black steed.

When she awoke and regained her senses, she found herself in the arms of a dark and handsome man, and asked him if he had seen the Demon Hunter. He told

---

37. Whitlock, Ralph. *The Folklore of Devon*, p.19.

her that he had not, but had himself be walking upon the cliffs alone in 'the grief of disappointed hope' when he had found her unconscious on the ground.

The young maid told the stranger of her woes, and he intimated unto her that revenge was possible. 'I would give my soul to have revenge' she blurted, unwittingly making a deal with the Devil, for that, of course, was the true identity of the dark stranger.

For many nights, he and she would meet and walk together upon those cliffs; plotting and nurturing her spite for the young man who had rejected her, and the girl he loved instead.

One evening, the pair spied the young couple approaching as they took a romantic walk together. The young maid rushed forth, and in a fury she stabbed them both to death. No sooner had she committed the terrible deed; her revenge attained, the Wild Hunt again could be heard as the Devil came to complete the deal. With his ghostly baying black hounds, he thundered forth on his mighty steed, snatched up the young maid as the hellish hunt drove onward over the cliff and down into the deep chasm of Daddy Hole. Of course, she was never seen again; for her soul had become his, forever.

On Sunday the 21st of October 1638, a terrible storm erupted at Widecombe-in-the-Moor, when the tower of the church of St Pancras was struck; it seems by 'ball lightening' during afternoon service. Many of the worshippers were badly injured, and some were killed. The cause was attributed to a visit by the Devil; to claim the soul of one of the congregation who had struck a bargain with him.

At 'The Devil's Rendezvous', a Bronze Age kist on Blacksdown Down, it was said that a man by the name John Reynolds went in 1631 to make a deal with the Devil. There, the Old One appeared to him, masked and wearing a hooded cloak. A deal was indeed struck, and Jan Reynolds told the Devil that if he should ever find him sleeping in church, then his soul was the Devil's to claim.

Seven years later, Jan nodded off during afternoon service at the church of St Pancras, and the Devil came swiftly to claim what was his; bringing with him the terrible storm that tore through the church that day.

In the delightful north Devon village of Shebbear, beneath a great oak tree, there rests a curious large boulder upon the neatly kept lawn of the village square. 'The Devil's Stone' as it is called, is the focus of the village's unique 5th of November ceremony, for every year the bells of the church of St Michael and All Angels, which sits nearby, are rung discordantly, and then the bell-ringers leave the church to gather around the stone, armed with long metal bars. The vicar will then tell the story of the Devil's stone, and then begins the 'Turning the Boulder' as the bell-ringers use all their strength to lift and turn the Devil's Stone.

According to local tradition, if the stone is not turned each year then misfortune will befall the village and its surrounding farms, as appears to have been the case when the stone went unturned during the Second World War.

One folkloric explanation for the need to turn the stone is that it fell upon the Devil during a battle with God, trapping him beneath it. In a bid to free himself, the Devil is said to dig downwards and up again to emerge the other side of the stone; a process which takes one year. However, the stone is of course turned over, re-trapping him, and his fruitless year-long dig begins again.

A lesser known but perhaps more mysterious Devonshire stone can be found immediately outside the Hare & Hounds Inn at Putts Corner, Sidbury. Almost hidden from view amongst the Inn's plants and shrubs is 'The Witches' Rock', also known as 'The Rolling Stone of Gittisham Common'. The stone has attached to it a tradition that witches would gather about it to perform rites of human sacrifice, and that they would offer to the stone the blood of their victims. The association with witches is perhaps particularly interesting given that the stone was once stood at four crossroads; a location often associated in folklore with witch rites and gatherings.

The name 'The Rolling Stone of Gittisham Common' is due to the tradition that the stone was possessed of some power enabling it to move, and that at midnight the stone would roll down to the River Sid to drink or bathe itself.

In addition to stones such as these, which may well have been deposited in their locations by the action of nature, Devonshire is also home to mysterious and folklore imbued stone structures, put together for spiritual purposes by ancient man. One such structure is the beautiful and enigmatic Spinsters Rock. Despite its name, this is not one rock, but four; the last remains of a Neolithic chamber tomb, known as a dolmen or a chromlech. These ancient burial structures would originally have been covered over with an earth mound, perhaps leaving an entrance, and the often quite enormous cap-stone exposed. Over millennia however the mounds erode away leaving mysterious giant 'boxes' of stone.

Our example, Spinsters Rock, sits in a beautiful field, part bordered by Ash and Oak trees on Shilstone Farm, Drewsteignton. The farm itself takes its name from the ancient cromlech; 'shilstone' meaning 'shelf-stone'.[38]

The dolmen, with its three upright stones supporting the large capstone, has been associated with local witches as well as the mythology of the three 'Fates'.[39]

This connection obviously relates to the name of the structure, and to a local tradition attached to it.

---

38. St Leger-Gordon, Ruth E. *The Witchcraft & Folklore of Dartmoor*, p.72-73.
39. Howard, Michael. *West Country Witches*, p.28.

The folklore states that three women, working as wool-spinsters, were responsible for erecting the monument. One day, whilst taking a break from their spinning wheels, they found entertainment in creating the structure; given the size and enormous weight of the stones involved, these must have been some rather extraordinary spinsters!

The creation of pre-historic structures, and of notable landscape features, is often associated in folklore with 'supernatural' beings such as the Devil, and of course giants, who themselves may possibly be folk-memories of ancient deities. It is perfectly reasonable therefor to accept at least the possibility that the three spinsters of Spinsters Rock, could in some way relate to the three Norns of Norse mythology; Urd, Verdandi, and Skuld; weavers of the fates of gods and men. Could Norsemen have seen this particular dolmen of three standing stones holding aloft the great capstone, and made an association with their three sisters of fate? The Vikings were, after all, present in Devonshire.[40]

Another tradition attached to Spinster's Rock, although unrelated to its name, tells of an elderly man and his three sons, who are said to have been Noah and his sons Shem, Ham and Japheth. One version of the tradition states that these were the builders of the dolmen, and another that they are themselves the stones; the capstone being Noah himself, supported by his three sons in old age, and that they were all turned to stone for some unknown offense; a punishment which the folklore of ancient stone monuments tells us was often meted out for the sin of dancing on the Sabbath.

Devonshire is also home to perhaps the most enigmatic kind of all ancient monuments; the stone circles. A particularly large and intact example is Scorhill Circle on Gidleigh Common, northeast of Dartmoor. The

---

40. Collingwood, W. G. *Scandinavian Britain*, p.98.

circle has gathered about it a somewhat eerie reputation, and visitors report feelings of an evil presence around the circle which is said to be inhabited by a 'troll' who devours sheep. Scorhill's reputation is heightened no doubt by reports from riders that their horses exhibit a mysterious fear of the ancient site; often refusing to walk upon the track that passes right through the stones, necessitating instead a detour around them.[41]

Scorhill Circle features in an interesting, if somewhat gruesome tradition of Chagford and its 'faithless wives'.

It is said that women and young maids who had shown themselves to be erring and fickle in their relationships could prove themselves worthy of forgiveness by performing an extraordinary rite encompassing four mysterious Dartmoor locations. First, they were to venture out to Cranmere 'Pool', which, in reality, is an area of treacherous boggy ground long said to be a place where mischievous ghosts and the souls of wrongdoers are bound in torment. Here the woman had to wash herself before continuing onto Scorhill Circle and there run three times around the stones.

From there the woman would go down to the Tolmen; a huge mass of rock with a large hole worn right through it by the action of water, and overhanging the Teign river. She would then have to clamber through this hole, before beginning the long walk to the pair of stone circles known as the Grey Wethers. Before one of the stones the woman then had to kneel, if by this point she managed not to collapse in exhaustion, and pray for forgiveness. If she were worthy, nothing would happen and the woman was free to return home and be forgiven by her community. If, however, her heart was deemed to be inherently unfaithful, the stone would topple forward; crushing her to death.[42]

---

41. St Leger-Gordon, Ruth E. *The Witchcraft & Folklore of Dartmoor*, p.72.
42. *Ibid*, p.60.

In this tradition do we merely have a moralistic 'warning' to the maids of Chagford to show themselves to be faithful in their relationships? Certainly, the prospect of having to carry out such a gruelling slog to and fro across moor should be a deterrent enough without the possibility of being crushed to death at the end of it. Or, do we have here the folk-survival or memory, probably highly corrupted by the passage of time, of some ancient form of landscape based ritual procession?

The Tolmen, the great holed stone featuring in this story, also has attached to it a tradition of ritual healing. It was said that people suffering from rheumatic complaints should climb upon the stone and drop themselves through the hole to receive both a cure and immunity from further suffering. One could speculate that this could possibly be a memory of older rituals associated with the stone.

Certainly the Tolmen continues to be a place of ritual to this day; Levannah Morgan in 'A Witch's Mirror' describes how the stone is visited by witches in Devonshire seeking initiation; instead of dropping themselves down through the hole, the witches go beneath the stone, climb up through the hole and out onto the stone's top. This is repeated three times.[43]

Evidence of modern era traditional witchcraft activities were uncovered at Soussons Common Circle, also known as the Ringastan, Runnage Circle, and Ephraim's Pinch. Although it has the appearance of a stone circle, of the kind believed to have been the venue for the ritual observances of ancient man, it is in fact what remains of the kerb of a long eroded cairn.

Soussons Common Circle was excavated in 1903 by the Barrow Committee, during which the central 'kist', a box-tomb constructed of stone, was uncovered. As the earth was carefully removed from its interior,

---

43. Morgan, Levannah. *A Witch's Mirror*, p.25.

to discover if any remains survived, a 'floor' of flat stones was found. It had been thought that this was the original bottom of the kist, however, when the stones were removed it was discovered that they were in fact a false floor, and that the original floor lay beneath; along with a curious find. Two coils of hair, which upon examination were found to be human, were found to have been placed in a cavity beneath the false floor. As the soil was highly acidic, there was no possibility that these coils of hair could have survived from pre-history, and were a much later, even fairly modern addition.

The general belief about these two coils of hair, is that they were the result of the survival of traditional witchcraft in Devonshire, and an act of sympathetic 'black magic' in order to cause the original owner of the hair a slow and wasting death.

It seems that the site remains a venue for ritual activity today, although of a less covert nature, for in the centre of this ring of stones there is often to be found the remains of a bonfire; particularly after the 'high nights' of the ritual year celebrated by neo-pagans. It seems that workers of ritual and magic today are often far less careful to conceal the evidence of their activities than the depositor of the locks of hair had been.

Cecil Williamson wrote about the importance of the remote places of the landscape and the ancient stone monuments within the work of the Devonshire witch. For example, he explains that the high and remote places of Dartmoor were ideal settings for the important work of contacting the spirit world. Getting to their working sites required a long and often difficult journey on foot, and so the local witches would travel light, and where possible, conceal heavier working implements so that they could remain at the place to be brought out upon the witch's arrival, and hidden again at the completion of their work.

In the collection of the Museum of Witchcraft and Magic is a slab of granite, intriguingly affixed with two differing pieces of granite; one reddish in colour, and another black and white. With it is exhibited a small earthenware jug, and before the devastating flood of 2004, it was accompanied also by a forked stick. Cecil's description card tells also of a pair of horn cups, and a fine white bone chalice, but these are no longer present either.

We are told the slab, and its associated objects, belonged to and were used by a Devonshire witch named Alice who lived in Ashburton. Her chosen place for working magic and communing with the spirit world was on Bench Tor, from where all three pieces of granite had originated.

The slab, Cecil explains, was used by Alice as an altar, and she kept it at her working place on the Tor; burying it in the ground after each working. The other implements she would carry with her, along with a flask in which she carried her home-brewed 'fairy honey wine' as well a box of matches with which Alice would kindle a fire made from gorse twigs, or 'furze' which she gathered from the Tor.

At the stone circles, Cecil Williamson's notes explain one of the uses to which the local witches would put these ancient structures, for it is here, he tells us, that they perform serpent-like 'maze dances' to aid their magic making; coiling in and out around the standing stones. The Maze dances, Cecil writes, re-tread the footsteps of the ancients, and are danced as an act of operative magic to bring about a beneficial result for the community.[44]

It is of course not only upon the lonely and desolate tor that the witches work, or at the sacred structures of ancient man, but also at the present-day structures of

44. Williamson, Cecil. Description card no.455, The Museum of Witchcraft & Magic.

religious worship. In Devonshire, as is indeed the case across the land, witches traditionally venture out by night to work their secret rites and their magic within and around churches and their yards.

Why this should be so is quite understandable; not only for the fact that many an old church is built upon a site of more ancient significance, but because they are naturally liminal places. In church, people come together to commune with the divine and observe sacred rituals of seasonal celebration, marriage, exorcism (for that is what baptismal rites essentially are) and death. The churchyard itself of course is the resting ground of the dead themselves, and is a location traditionally associated with strange spirits, folk-divinatory observances, and even the presence of the Devil.

One Devonshire burial ground, where evidence of occult ritual activity has been found, is Score Wood Cemetery Near Illfracombe. This is a cemetery and chapel which was long abandoned and overgrown, however the chapel itself, once a rather spooky and notorious ruin, has since been sold off and converted into a rather smart house. Locals, many of whom have loved ones interred there, are currently campaigning to have the cemetery, which is still in a very neglected state and closed off from public access, reopened and properly maintained.

During the chapel's time as an eerie ruin, local youngsters were known to go there at night to dabble in the occult, as well as to engage in the usual drinking, smoking and vandalism, away from adult eyes. However, in addition to the youthful casual experiments by the supernaturally curious, there is evidence that the site may have been the location for occult practices of a far more serious and refined nature. Not long ago, interments occasionally were still made in the overgrown cemetery, and on one such occasion workmen discovered the scene of what appears to have been the setting of an elaborate witchcraft ritual. Two perfect circles had been marked out on the ground, the larger of the two being six foot in diameter. Inside this a hexagram, or six-pointed star had been marked out, again perfectly and geometrically correct. The left-over stumps of several black candles were carefully arranged and strange daubs of black, green and white pigment were placed here and there. This seems unlikely to have been the work of dabbling youths, nor does it sound as though followers of the modern wiccan Craft were responsible. Could these twin 'working circles' have been the work of some band of ceremonial magicians, or perhaps a West Country coven of traditional witches?

Witches and the Devil are not the only encounters one might make within the Devonshire landscape, for this is a land heavily populated by spirits, particularly by the tribe of spirit folk known as the Pixies. Perhaps 'spirit' is not really the correct term, for the Pixies might well be creatures of a mysteriously liminal nature; not entirely spirit, but neither entirely of flesh but occupying a state that lies somewhere betwixt the two.

Like their neighbours across the River Tamar; the Cornish Piskies, The Devonshire Pixies are not easy to find for they are notoriously shy and exhibit a disliking for being observed by human kind. They prefer to make their homes away from the hustle and bustle of man; in the remote and wild places, within rocks, caves and earth hollows.

The Pixie is however not entirely ill-disposed towards humankind, and is seen to have particular sympathy for the poor, and those engaged in hard, thankless labour. Odd tasks, about the farm or household, might mysteriously be found to have been completed in the night by unseen hands. Such beneficial relationships with the Pixies have traditionally been encouraged by old Devon folk who would provide them a little comfort by leaving a basin of clean water for the Pixies by the fire.[45]

---

45. Whitlock, Ralph. *The Folklore of Devon*, p.29.

One must remember however that, if care is not taken, the Pixies could be easily offended, and there are various taboos which must be observed. For example, the Pixies take offense at being thanked for any tasks they complete on behalf of a human, or news of any kindness they show being shared with others. They despise being spied upon by humans, and exhibit a particular dislike of greed, promiscuity, and laziness in one's labours. Much mischief is likely to ensue if such behaviour occurs when Pixies are around.

There are of course certain rocks and landscape features associated with the Devonshire Pixies, and caves appear to be a favourite dwelling place.

Low upon Dartmoor's granite strewn Sheepstor is a large cubical mass of stacked stone in the midst of which is a narrow opening known as the Pixie's Cave. Here, it is said, that Pixies make their home, and that one can sometimes hear them hard at work with their busy hammering echoing from deep within; for they are said to be great crafters of metal. To the Pixie's Cave, people would bring offerings; which traditionally took the form of a bunch of grass, a few pins, or a piece of cloth large enough for the Pixies to fashion clothing from.

'Tracey Bovey', writing in *The Cauldron*, tells us that on midnight, at the full moon, anyone brave enough to go there would see the Pixies come out of the cave to dance in the moon's light. We are also told that the cave was originally used as a tomb, and that the bodies of ancient warriors holding bronze swords were placed here to rest. However, if Britain were ever in danger, the warriors would arise from their tomb to come to her defence.[46]

At Chudleigh Rocks, close to the edge of Dartmoor and the Teign Valley, is another cave said to be a Pixie dwelling place. Like the Pixie's Cave on Sheepstor, 'Pixie's Hole' is associated with ancient man, and yields evidence

---

46. Bovey, Tracy. 'Weird Tales of Old Dartmoor', *The Cauldron* No.140, p.25.

that reveals the cave to have been occupied and used by humans from the Upper Palaeolithic. Such associations are interesting for it has been suggested that certain tribes of the fairy race could either be memories of ancient man, or their spirits; occupying a spiritual dimension of the landscape, just beyond normal perception.

Old Pixie lore concerning offerings, the taking of children, and of walkers becoming 'pixie-led', surrounds Chudleigh Rocks and the Pixie's Hole. Just as at Sheepstor, and other dwelling places of the Pixies, pins were left as a traditional offering. Within Pixie's Hole there was a certain rock known as 'The Devil's Pincushion', or for the anti-papists, 'The Pope's Head'. It was evidently fairly soft in nature, for visitors to the cave would bring pins with them to stick into the stone as a propitiatory offering to the 'elfin inhabitants'.[47]

The tradition of changelings, in which the fairy folk are said to take away human babies and small children, and leaving an infant of their own kind in its place is well known. However, the Pixies of Chudleigh Rocks seemed content to abduct, without necessarily bothering with replacements.

A couple, who lived not far from the Pixie's Hole, had two children, and one morning, after dressing their eldest, the mother let her run off to play while she dressed the baby. Some time passed however, with no sign of their daughter, and so, becoming very worried, the couple enlisted the help of their neighbours to find her. For days they searched to no avail and bloodhounds were sent for in the hope that her scent may be followed.

However, one morning, a group of youths went collecting nuts from trees close to the keeper's house when they came upon the little girl, undressed but apparently happy and well, and merrily playing with

---

47. Lloyd Warden Page, John. *The Rivers of Devon from Source to Sea*, P.82.

some toads, or it may have been her toes; the collector of this story was unsure which, possibly due to strong Devonian accents!

So strong was the belief in the Chudleigh Rocks Pixies' fondness for spiriting away young children (to the extent that local mothers would sleep with their infants tied to them in bed), that all remained firmly convinced that it was the Pixies who had taken, and later returned the child.[48]

The usual Pixie mischief of leading travellers astray has also been recorded at Chudleigh Rocks. In a 19th century account, the victim, a man making his way home on a moonlit night, 'full of strong drink', passed over the hill above the Pixie's Hole. As he did so he heard a strange and inexplicable, yet sweet music, and found himself being led from his path into a 'whirling dance' by the 'good folk'. Without mercy, they delighted in spinning the man round and round until he fell to the ground. Eventually, he came to his senses and was able to find his path and return home, where he retired to his bed, never to leave it again for he died a short while later.[49]

The Queen of the Fairy tribes herself is said to have used her magical powers in Devon to create a bridge near Tavistock. Writing in 1846, Rachel Evens explains;

'South-down bridge is just suited to be the resort of the fairies or of some such aerial beings. In a certain tale written to illustrate the gleaming beauty of the scene, a supernatural origin is thus given to the bridge; "The queen of the fairies proceeded with her wondering train to the borders of the clear stream, bending over the font for one moment, she gazed musingly upon its pellucid waters; then gathering together a portion of the liquid store, she flung it high into the air; the drops descending caught the rays of the pale

48. Northcote, Lady Rosalind. 'Devonshire Folk-lore', *Folklore* No.11, p.213.

49. H.G.T. *Pixies or Piskies, Notes & Queries* No.61, p.510.

moon, and formed a rainbow. "For ever, for ever," repeated Ina, waving her sceptre over the glittering bow. Stopped in its course the falling moisture remained suspended in the air, touching on either side the shelving banks of the stream. Gradually it changed its form, stones of mighty size replaced the trembling drops, and with wonder and delight the fairies beheld – a bridge. Then arose a shout of joy from the elfin crew; they bounded on the object of their admiration; they decked it with moss and fern; they hid themselves in frolic beneath its spreading arch."' [50]

---

50. Evens, Rachel. *Home Scenes: or, Tavistock and its Vicinity*, p.67-68.

LADY HOWARD

BLACK DOGS & WILD HUNTERS

Spectral Black Dogs abound in Devonshire folklore. For most people, the subject will conjure thoughts of Sir Henry Baskerville being stalked across the mist-shrouded moor by a huge phosphorescent hound; such is the enduring legacy of Sir Arthur Conan Doyle's most beloved Sherlock Holmes mystery. Whilst there are no legends of centuries old family curses unleashing a demon-dog to pursue the head of the household to his death, there are established traditions of ghostly packs of hellish hounds that chase lone travellers, as well as solitary

Black Dog apparitions; often heavily associated with the dead. So, for Sir Arthur Conan Doyle, Dartmoor will have been a rich source of inspiration, as well as providing a fittingly 'gothic' setting for his masterpiece.

The link between Black Dog apparitions and the dead is perhaps not a surprising one, given that dogs of a corporeal nature also share this association. The dog itself was seen as a creature of omen; foretelling death. It was long believed that dogs possessed the ability to see Death, as well as spirits, and would begin to howl outside a house where one of the occupants was dying.[51]

In Devonshire folklore, the Black Dog apparition is particularly associated with the ghosts of deceased people; perhaps most famously with the phantom of Lady Howard.

Born at Fitzford House in 1596, Lady Mary Howard was the daughter of Sir John Fitz, who in Devonshire folklore is associated with two holy wells; both having attached to them the tale that he and his wife Bridget Courtenay had discovered them after becoming 'pixie lead'. A dense mist shrouded the couple, and they were unable to find their way. Becoming tired as they continued round and round in fruitless circles, they stumbled upon a spring, and as soon as they refreshed themselves with its waters, the mists vanished and the pixie spell was broken.

One of the wells, just outside Princetown, is named Fice's Well and was preserved by Sir John Fitz with the erection of a granite well house. It is inscribed '*IF* [John Fitz] *1568*'. The other, 'Ftiz's Well' near Okehampton, was marked by the erection of a stone cross.[52]

Sir John Fitz was, by all accounts, not a liked man for he was a notorious drunk of violent temper and guilty of at

---

51. Norman, Mark. *Black Dog Folklore*, p.127.
52. St. Leger-Gordon, Ruth E. *The Witchcraft & Folklore of Dartmoor*, p.19.

least two murders. Following the second murder, which he committed whilst en route to London to account for his appalling behaviour, he took his own life by stabbing himself twice.

At only nine years old, his daughter Mary inherited his fortune, and would enter into four marriages. The first occurred after she was made a ward by King James I to the Earl of Northumberland, who later married her off to his brother Sir Allan Percy. She never lived with him however, as Sir Allan died before she came of age; he caught a 'severe chill' after having rested on damp ground when hot and tired from hunting.[53]

Her second marriage was apparently for love, for she eloped to wed a Thomas Darcy, however he sadly died not long after the wedding. Mary's third marriage, to Sir Charles Howard, would also end prematurely in her becoming yet again a widow in 1626.

Her fourth marriage, which bore her two children, was not to last long for she would separate from Sir Richard Grenville in 1631.

In time, Lady Howard's reputation would become conflated with that of her father's, and suspicion grew around the deaths of her husbands, until in folklore she was portrayed as having been a cruel woman, of ill-temper, who murdered all four of them.

For these misdeeds in life, Devonshire folklore tells us that she was doomed to do penance in spirit and unable to rest. There are a few differing versions of this penance, mostly recorded in the 19th century, and all involving the apparition of a Black Dog.

In some versions, Lady Howard takes the form of a black hound and is doomed each midnight to run from the gateway of Fitzford House to Okehampton Park. There she must pluck a single blade of grass and return with it in her mouth, to Fitzford, before cock-crowing.

---

53. Baring-Gould, Sabine. *Devonshire Characters & Strange Events*, p.195.

This task she was doomed to carry out every night, and until every single blade of grass had been plucked from the park, at which point the world will come to its end.

In other versions, Lady Howard's ghost rides in a coach made of bones, some say the bones of her four husbands (variously towards the moor, from Fitzford to Okehampton Castle to collect the blade of grass and back again, or between Okehampton Castle and Launceston Castle), preceded by a black hound breathing fire (in some variants the hound is cyclopean). If the ghostly coach stopped at a door, there would be a death in that house that very night.[54]

The Rev. Sabine Baring-Gould speculates that the story of Lady Howard's 'Death Coach' could be a memory of the 'Goddess of Death travelling over the world collecting human souls.'[55] Folklorist Mark Norman (author of *Black Dog Folklore*; the most comprehensive study of the Black Dog phenomenon, sightings and traditions), suggests the possibility that the Journey of Lady Howard, in her coach or in the form of a black hound, may have been superimposed upon an earlier tradition of a Black Dog haunting, for such are often associated with old roads and trackways.[56]

Another tradition of a human ghost transformed into a Black Dog is associated with Dean Combe Valley, near Mary Tavy. When a weaver, by the name of Knowles, passed away, he remained so devoted to his craft that his ghost returned to his loom and continued to work. His family, much annoyed and frightened by this manifestation, called upon the services of a conjuring parson to perform an exorcism.

---

54. Baring-Gould, Sabine. *Devonshire Characters & Strange Events*, p.209-210.

55. *Ibid*, p.211.

56. Norman, Mark. *Black Dog Folklore*, p.43.

With great difficulty, the parson managed to draw the ghost of Weaver Knowles away from his beloved loom, and into the churchyard. Here, the spirit was transformed into a phantom Black Dog when the parson cast over him a handful of churchyard earth. The parson then bound Weaver Knowles to a basin in the Dean Burn; the stream running through the Combe. Here, Knowles, in the form of a phantom hound, was set the unending task of emptying the pool with a perforated nutshell. To this day, in the beautiful Dean Combe, there remains a basin known as Hound's Pool.[57]

The old association between the Black Dog and the dead, is seen in some of the locations Black Dog apparitions are traditionally said to haunt. These include old gallows sites, the scenes of murders, graves and churchyards.[58]

There are a number of ancient burial mounds, gravesites and cairns on Exmoor and the Blackdown Hills, and these sites are associated with Black Dog sightings. One, the Wembarrow Dog, would appear when hunting parties rode too close to the ancient cairns; linking the apparition with both the ancient dead and the landscape.[59]

We find also a link with Black Dog apparitions and gravesites of a more recent kind in the old tradition of the Church Grim; the guardian of the churchyard. An explanation as to why the Church Grim traditionally manifests as a Black Dog has been suggested by some who link it to the tradition of the first burial. It was the old belief that the soul of the first to be interred in a churchyard would thereafter be bound to the place, in order to watch over and protect the other burials. To

---

57. St. Leger-Gordon, Ruth E. *The Witchcraft & Folklore of Dartmoor*, p.54.

58. Norman, Mark. *Black Dog Folklore*, p.129.

59. *Ibid*, p.131.

circumvent a human having to take on this task, it was said that a dog would be interred first instead, and that its ghost would become the Church Grim.[60]

This practice would appear to be reminiscent of the concealment of animals as apotropaic charms within the fabric of buildings, most commonly occurring in the form of cats intentionally positioned within walls, or horse skulls concealed beneath floorboards.

As we shall later see though, the relationship between dogs and human burials is far more ancient than the apotropaic burial of dogs in churchyards.

Liminality would seem to be a key aspect of the locations where Black Dog apparitions occur; burials being a point of liminality between the living and the dead, this world and the Otherworld. The most extensive collection of Black Dog sightings and experiences was published by Mark Norman in 2016. In this collection, he estimates that one third of these are accounts of apparitions occurring at roads, lanes, footpaths and bridges. These locations too are intrinsically liminal in nature; being passages betwixt one place and another. Flowing water is a notorious location of folkloric liminality, and so too are the bridges that cross them.

A particularly interesting lane associated apparition was known in the village of Uplyme, right on the Devon-Dorset border. A Black Dog is said to haunt Haye Lane, which was previously known as Black Dog Lane, for it is here that the apparition walks in silence; crossing the border at midnight.

A bizarre sighting of this apparition took place in 1856, when a 'sober-minded woman and her husband were walking the lane. The woman saw a large, black and 'shaggy' dog approaching them, and as it did so it grew dramatically in size to become as tall as the trees, and finally dispersed like a mist. Her husband however saw

---

60. Norman, Mark. *Black Dog Folklore*, p.132.

only a 'vapour from the sea'. The woman reported that the dog she saw had 'fiery eyes' and that it caused the air to be 'cold and dank'.[61]

The particular habits of the Uplyme Black Dog; the crossing of the Devon-Dorset border, and the timing of midnight, are additional and potent examples of liminality.

Another dog, associated with the themes of roads and midnight, occurs at Yealmbridge, about eight miles from Plymouth. At midnight, under a full moon, and at a spot not far from the bridge, the Black Dog appears and walks in silence; eventually to disappear on the Egloskerry road.[62]

A dramatic encounter with a Black Dog was experienced by a man walking across the moor from Princetown to Plymouth one winter in the 19th century. On the latter part of his long walk, the man found himself accompanied by a Black Dog of unusually large size. He tried to give his new travel companion a kind pat on the head, but found to his astonishment that his hand passed right through! And so he continued, with his otherworldly escort by his side, until the pair drew close to Plymouth, when suddenly, there was a flash and an almighty crash, and the man fell unconscious by the side of the road. He was not found and given help until the next morning.

A folkloric explanation for this particular Black Dog tells us that long ago, a traveller was murdered upon the spot where the man in our story fell unconscious, and that the ghost of his faithful dog patrols the road, looking for his killer in the hope of taking their life.[63]

When Cecil Williamson was running his witchcraft museum on the Isle of Man, he naturally became aware

---

61. Norman, Mark. *Black Dog Folklore*, p.46.

62. Whitlock, Ralph. *The Folklore of Devon*, p.61.

63. *Ibid*, p.60-61.

of the Manx traditions of the Mogah-doo. This was the black hound of death omens, and if it sat outside a cottage, howling, it foretold that a death in the family was approaching.

Cecil would later however have an encounter of his own with a Black Dog of Devonshire. He possessed a keen interest in the investigation of locations with mysterious or magical associations, and so, one still night in 1972, Cecil made his way up to the tomb of Squire Cabell in the churchyard of Buckfastleigh Church. There, arriving at his chosen spot at three o'clock in the morning; his favourite time 'for dealing with out-of-this-world subjects', he drank in the silence of the night and waited.

Buckfastleigh Church, and its yard, has long been associated with witchcraft meetings and dark occult practices, debris often having been found left at the site in evidence of secret nocturnal activities. Such activity is thought to have resulted in the fire which consumed the interior of the church in 1992, leaving only the stone walls standing as an eerie ruin today. It is said that the Devil can be conjured by walking seven times around the church, after which his horned face will appear in the porch.

Back though to Cecil's churchyard vigil. After about half an hour, a black dog with long hair, and the appearance of a large Labrador, approached. Sensing perhaps that Cecil was a dog lover, he came to rest his head in Cecil's lap for a bit of fuss. This dog seemed to Cecil to be no spectral hound, for it was warm, and solidly corporeal to the touch. After some time, the dog put his front paws on Cecil's lap in order to give him a big lick on the face, and, as would be the natural reaction from any dog lover, Cecil gave the dog a hug in return. Another friendly lick was given, and another hug attempted, but this time Cecil's arms went right through the dog as it vanished into thin air! He described the feeling as being 'like crushing a blown-up paper bag'.[64]

It was during a meeting in London of the Folklore Society, that Cecil Williamson met the anthropologist and Egyptologist Margaret Murray, who introduced him to Anubis; 'the black dog-god of the Ancient Egyptian Underworld.'

Through research and a visit to Egypt, Cecil became something of an 'Anubis fan' and always kept an active shrine in his home to 'the Egyptian Black Dog'.

Via Anubis, we have a particularly ancient correlation of the Black Dog with the themes of death, the dead and the underworld, first arising perhaps from the ancient Egyptians observing desert Jackals, and their tendency to frequent cemeteries; digging up and feeding on the corpses buried there.

Other ancient associations can be found in Greek Mythology and Cerberus; the tri-headed 'Hound of Hades', guarding the gates of the underworld, and thus, the souls of the dead. Also, perhaps Geri and Freki; the wolf companions of the Germanic god Odin; a leader, amongst others, of the Wild Hunt.

It is this phenomena that brings us from the solitary Black Dog apparitions that haunt the tombs, lanes, roads and tracks of the Devonshire landscape, to the terrible packs of Otherworld hounds that ride forth with the Wild Hunt.

This cross-cultural tradition has a particularly strong presence in the folklore of Devonshire, where many a traveller across the moors has heard the terrible baying of the hunt's hounds (known in the South West as the 'Yeth Hounds', and the 'Wish' or 'Wisht Hounds'), along with the thundering hooves of its horses and the blasting horn of the dark hunter himself. There are various

---

64. Williamson, Cecil. 'Close Encounter with a Demon Hound', *The Caudron* No.78, p.12.

identities attributed to this dark figure, who leads the ghostly hunt across the stormy skies of winter; often in Devon, as we have seen in previous chapters, he is said to be the Devil, and sometimes the reputed witch Sir Francis Drake.

Another candidate in Devonshire tradition however is the notorious Squire Cabell. Living in the 17th century, Cabell, a keen huntsman, had gained quite a sinister reputation; he was regarded as an intrinsically wicked man, he was rumoured to have committed murder, and to have sold his soul to the Devil.

His death in 1677 has attached to it various stories, including that it was caused by his own pack of hunting hounds who savaged him and went on to live wild on the moor, or that it was the wild hunt itself; its Wisht Hounds chasing him across the moor until he dropped dead.[65]

It was in the churchyard of Holy Trinity Church, Buckfastleigh, where Squire Cabell's body was interred, and where of course Cecil Williamson had encountered his own 'demon hound'. However, on the night of his burial, it is said that the dark Wisht Hounds arrived to circle his tomb; baying for Cabell's soul to arise and lead them on their otherworldly hunt over the moor.

It is said the people of Buckfastleigh were so afraid of the Squire's restless and wicked soul that they made extra precautions against the arising of his ghost. They laid a great and heavy slab of stone over the squire's head, constructed an 'altar tomb' above this, and then encased the entire thing in what looks very much like a prison cell, complete with a heavy locked door of oak, and iron railings. Here, perhaps, we find an example of the old beliefs surrounding the magical properties of iron and its ability to bar the way against evil spirits.

Further traditions arose around the tomb building itself, such as that if one were to walk around it, some

---

65. Norman, Mark. *Black Dog Folklore*, p.51.

say thirteen times, some say seven, some say only once or even backwards, and then insert a finger into the keyhole of the door, or a hand through the iron bars, then you will feel the ghost of Squire Cabell, or the Devil Himself, nibbling upon it.

Shadowy 'demonic' forms are said to be seen, and to this day 'ghost hunting' groups visit the tomb in the dead of night, hoping to catch manifestations and mysterious red glowing lights, in and around the tomb, on their cameras.

The themes of death and passage to and from the Otherworld are central to the tradition of the Wild Hunt. Unbaptised children it seems were a common quarry of the hunt; perhaps a folkloric warning to get one's children baptised as soon as possible, but also perhaps, in the days of high child mortality rates, it tells something of the Wild Huntsman's role as psychopomp; ferrying the souls of the dead from this world to the next.

Such themes may be seen in the story of a Dartmoor farmer who encountered the Wild Hunt whist returning one night from Widdecombe Fair. Rather bravely, or perhaps foolishly, as the ghostly pack of black hounds and their dark master rode past him, the farmer called out, asking what success the huntsman had had that night, and if he might have some of his game. The huntsman turned and flung to the farmer a small sack, which landed at his feet. He continued home with his prize, only to find that, upon opening the sack, it contained the lifeless body of his own small child.[66]

The reputed 'stable' and setting-off point for the Wild Hunt on Dartmoor is the achingly mysterious Wistman's Wood; itself surrounded by hauntings and historical processions of the dead.

Running past the northern end of the wood is the Lych Way; a 'corpse-road' or 'way-of-the-dead'. It

---

66. Westwood, Jennifer. *Albion – A Guide to Legendary Britain*, p.39-41.

is upon this ancient 'ghost road' that the dead of the remote tenements and farms of Dartmoor were carried across the moor, for burial at Lydford prior to 1260, after which the dead could be interred at Widecombe. Sightings continue of ghostly hooded figures walking in procession along the 'way of the dead' to this day.

Wistman's Wood itself clings to the western face of a lonely valley slope above the rock-strewn River Dart. A mysterious, and otherworldly place, associated with stories of druidic rites; the wood is said to be haunted by the ghosts of ancient druid priests and home to many adders, hiding amongst the countless moss-covered boulders; strewn and piled amid the distorted oaks.

Devonshire witch, Jo O'Cleirigh, highlighted the ancient link between adders and the druids; one name for this mysterious priesthood is 'Nadredd' meaning 'adders'.[67]

There are various theories surrounding the origins of this wood's intriguing name. One possibility of course is that it relates to the West Country term 'wisht' meaning 'eerie' or 'uncanny', and therefor connected with the 'Wish' or 'Wisht Hounds' for whom Wistman's Wood is a kind of home, or perhaps a gateway between the worlds from where they go forth to hunt across the moor. 'Wistman' also appears interestingly to be a local name for the Devil; a most traditional candidate for the Wild Hunt's leadership.[68]

As an innately 'otherworldly' place, clinging to the edge of a valley, beside the flow of water, this is a wood which could be seen to be particularly liminal in nature. Those liminal times of dusk, dawn, and midnight, as well as the seasonal 'high nights' such as May Eve, and

---

67. O'Cleirigh, Jo. 'Milpreves or Adder's Beads', *Meyn Mamvro* No.1.
68. Westwood, Jennifer. *Albion – A Guide to Legendary Britain*, p.39.

Devonshire Image Magic. Above: images of a man, a woman, and body parts used in curative 'pin-pricking magic' in Crediton. Below: image magic of a darker kind from Exeter. Examples housed in the Museum of Witchcraft & Magic.

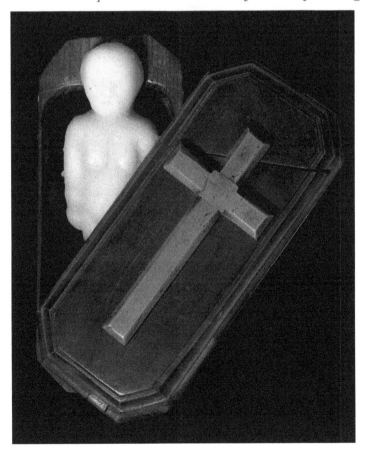

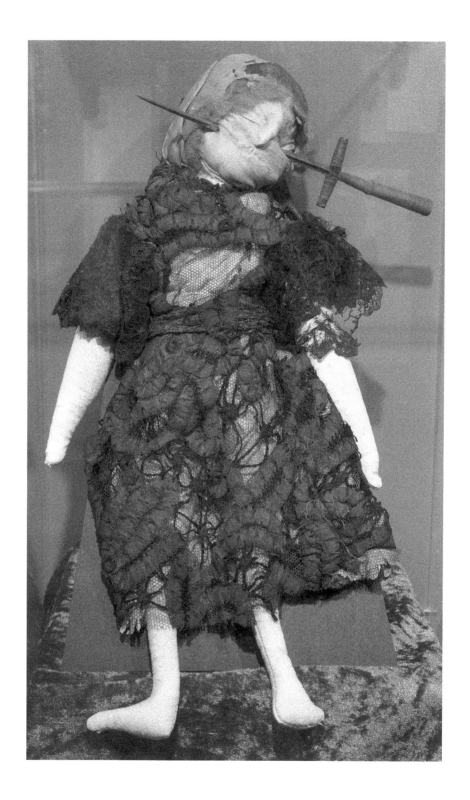

Facing page: a poppet made in Exmouth to curse a 'mean and spiteful' woman.

Above: 'Miss Wagging-Tongue', image magic from Paignton to silence a village gossip and scandal-monger.

Right: a poppet representing a woman and stuck with pins, found in Cecil Williamson's home after his death in 1999.

All housed in the Museum of Witchcraft & Magic.

Facing: photograph with edges burnt in an act of 'leave my husband alone' magic from Exeter. Above: plate, nest and bird skulls found in the roof of a Noss Mayo cottage in 1968. Below: a red shoe and wax encased stuffed sparrow, a curse charm prepared for a client by 'Black Dorris' in Plymouth. All in the Museum of Witchcraft & Magic.

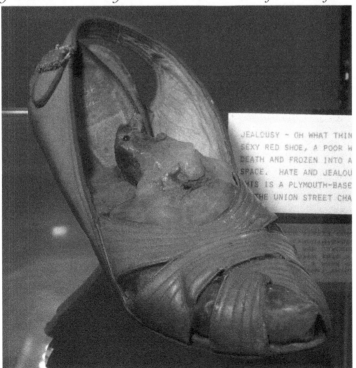

JEALOUSY - OH WHAT THIN
SEXY RED SHOE, A POOR W
DEATH AND FROZEN INTO A
SPACE.   HATE AND JEALOU
HIS IS A PLYMOUTH-BASE
THE UNION STREET CHA

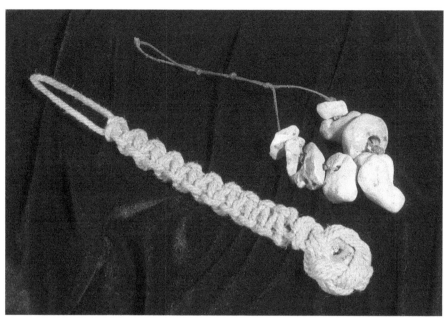

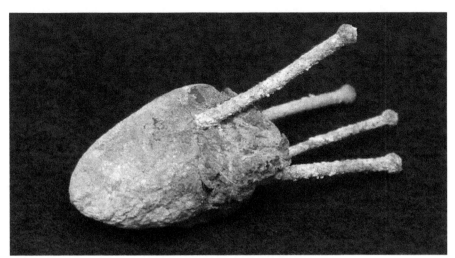

Facing, top: hag stones on knotted string, a charm, prepared by a Bridestowe witch to protect horses from being 'night ridden'. A beautiful hag stone and rope charm of the kind used in Devon to protect a boat from being 'witched'. Museum of Witchcraft & Magic.

Facing, bottom: nail and pin stuck sheep's heart, a counter-curse from South Devon. Clarke Collection.

Above: pin stuck seagull's heart counter curse, also from South Devon. Clarke Collection.

Right: dog's heart stuck with pins and left on the path to Cecil Williamson's house. Museum of Witchcraft & Magic.

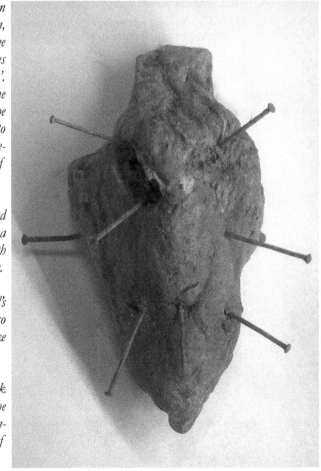

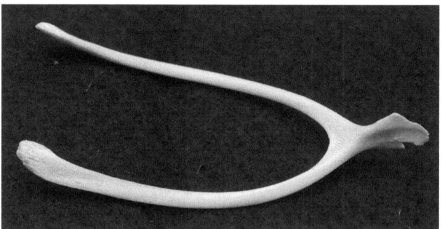

Wish bone, or 'merry thought' kept in Devon against drowning. Below: Three bees and a leather pouch, a Devonshire good fortune charm.

A garden swing, owned by Cecil Williamson. He described their use by witches in Devon and Cornwall to curse or to bless.

Below: Cecil's 'Pixy Pyramid' in his Devonshire garden. A curious device employing four of Cecil's favourite magical tools, wind, smoke, fire, and direction. Photo courtesy of Graham King.

A 'witch mirror' of the kind favoured by Cecil Williamson for spirit communication and protective magic. Author's collection.

Facing: a toad's remains and metal contraption of hooks and human faces. Found in the chimney of a house in Axminster in 1936, and interpreted as a curse charm. Museum of Witchcraft & Magic.

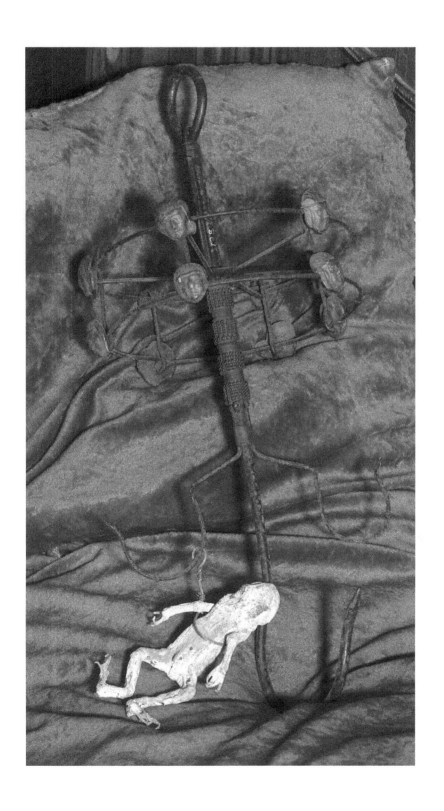

Charm bags containing the dried bodies of toads hung in Devonshire cottages 'to keep out witches'. Clarke Collection.

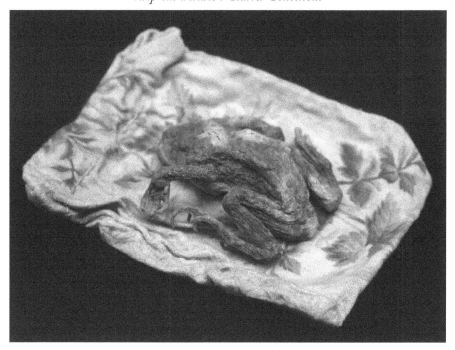

Midsummer Eve, have also been termed 'wisht' and regarded as potent times for working acts of magic or charming.[1]

'Tracy Bovey', writing in *The Cauldron*, suggests the interesting possibility that, in old British, the name might derive from 'wist' and 'maen' to mean a place of 'eerie stones', which it most certainly is.[2]

Adding yet further to the eerie regard with which Dartmoor is held, are the stories of 'Old Crockern'. This spectral figure is said to be the very *genius loci* of Dartmoor and to haunt Crockern Tor. He appears to be an old spirit or deity associated with the landscape, and death mysteries, for he is described as riding a skeletal horse glowing mysteriously with a green luminosity, carrying a great blade in the form of either a scythe or a sword. He is grey as the granite and his eyebrows shaggy as the mosses and ancient lichens that adorn both rock and wind distorted branch; as though he were made of the moor itself. Old Crockern is, by tradition, another of the leaders of the Wild Hunt; riding forth in the harsh winds over Dartmoor. His approach is heralded by the shrill whistling of icy cold wind and the mysterious rattling of bones.[3]

Ghostly Black Dogs and the Wild Hunt are also associated with witchcraft. Cecil Williamson spoke to Michael Howard about an existing witch tradition he was aware of which operated within the Bampton and Dulverton areas near Exmoor and was connected in some way with the ghostly manifestation of the Black Dog and the Wild Hunt. These two villages are particularly noted for their historical associations with stag hunting.[4]

---

1. Caple, John. *Somerset*, p.30.

2. Bovey, Tracey. 'Weird Tales of Dartmoor', *The Cauldron* No.140, p.20.

3. *Ibid*, p.20.

4. Howard, Michael. *West Country Witches*, p.47.

One of the Devil's favourite bestial forms, when manifesting before witches and presiding over the 'witches' sabbat', was the Black Dog. Witches in 17th century Argyll for example, were lead by a black dog with a chain about its neck, the tinkling sounds of which they followed to find their way to their nocturnal meetings.[5]

As well as Black Dogs though, Dartmoor, like Bodmin Moor in Cornwall, is today the setting for many an 'alien big cat' sighting. Many who have seen these creatures describe them as resembling such things as black panthers, pumas and even lions. Some of these creatures may indeed be escaped or released exotic pets (following the Dangerous Wild Animals Act of 1976), or zoo and circus escapees; for footprints identified by experts as belonging to various species of 'big cat' have been found, and the carcases of cattle, sheep and ponies have also been discovered, appearing to show signs of having been killed by 'big cats'. Whilst there may indeed be actual 'big cats' living and hunting on Dartmoor, many believe that some of the reported sightings of 'beasts' might be supernatural in nature, and simply a continuation of the old Dartmoor traditions of mysterious and otherworldly creatures. In the past, where a large mysterious dark creature was sighted upon the moor, the natural explanation would have been an encounter with one of the moor's spectral Black Dogs. Today, such otherworldly things are not so present in the consciousness of the majority of modern folk, and so the sighting of a dark creature is now far more likely to be put down to being that of an escaped and corporeal black panther.

On the moor today though, there are occasionally still those who attribute their strange beast sightings to the supernatural, rather than to the 'alien big cats'. On the ninth of June 2007, A Devon born professional falconer,

---

5. Gary, Gemma. 'The Man in Black', *Hands of Apostasy*, p.192-193

named Martin Whitley, took a group of American clients to Hound Tor. As he was flying a Hawk the group spotted a large blackish-grey creature which appeared to them to have strange 'shape-shifting' qualities; changing from 'feline' to 'bear-like' movement and form. Several photos were taken which appear to show the creature taking a slightly different form from frame to frame in which the creature's appearance seems to shift strangely between feline, bear-like, canine, and even resembling a wild boar.[6]

The fact that this strange sighting took place at the base of Hound Tor makes it very tempting indeed to link the occurrence with the Dartmoor Black Dog traditions. However, the culprit just may have been a Dartmoor black dog of a more corporeal nature, for a woman living not far from the location of the sighting, owns a large black Newfoundland dog named Troy, who is apparently allowed to explore the location alone and at his leisure, which, given the presence of armed 'big cat' hunters out on the moor, is probably not the best of ideas. His owner is utterly convinced that Troy is the 'supernatural' creature captured in the images, whilst the falconer Martin Whitely is equally adamant that the creature he and his party observed was not a dog of any breed. Thus the mystery of Dartmoor's strange beasts lives on.

6. Bovey, Tracey. 'Weird Tales of Dartmoor', *The Cauldron* No.140, p.22.

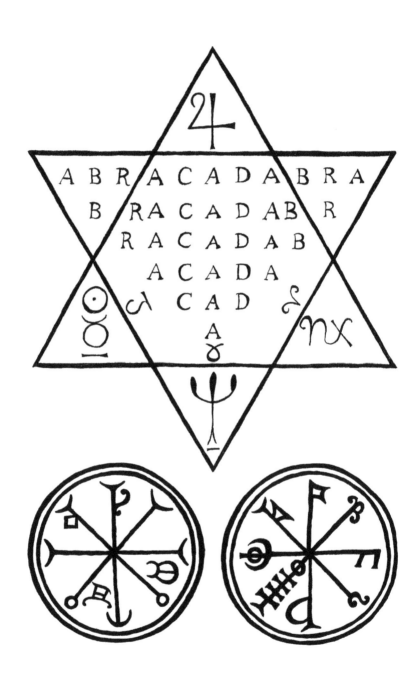

A BLACK BOOK *of* DEVONSHIRE MAGIC

Today in Devonshire, amidst its green and rolling landscape of hidden valley's, secretive woods, small village communities and remote farmsteads, one cannot help but feel that old and clandestine forms of witchcraft might, here and there, continue to be practiced unseen. Not so long ago though, in the 19th century and before, there would have been no need to suppose; for witches, working their arts for both good or ill, would seem to have been plentiful. The old beliefs in witchcraft, and the presence of spirits, amongst the ordinary people thrived; as noted by Sarah Hewett writing in 1898; 'Dwellers in the hilly parts of Devon, on Dartmoor and Exmoor, and in the villages bordering upon them, are as deeply imbued with faith in witches, as their forefathers were in the days when Alfred was king.'

The strength of such beliefs not only kept the 'white witches' well occupied in their trade, but nurtured a popular 'folk-magic', in which an array of traditional charms, spells and rites might be resorted to remedy the ills and woes of daily life.

Handed down to us from a time of unknown distance, and once lovingly recorded in the traditional 'black books' of the 'white witches', is a repository of magical lore in the form of written and spoken charms, inscribed vellum talismans, powders and preparations of herbs, woods and roots, and the bones, teeth, and other bodily parts of various animals and of humans.

In order to work their magic for the needs of their client, the witches of Devonshire, it seems, would gather about themselves a range of tools, many of which perhaps would have been natural items; gathered from field, wood, shore and hedgerow. For Cecil Williamson, nature itself was one of the witch's most potent tools; via the use, for example, of wind and smoke, as well as the 'spirit force' of streams.

Numerous tools associated with Devonshire witchery were displayed in Cecil's Museum of Witchcraft, some of which present something of a mystery as to how they might have been used. One such example is a strange disk of sandstone from Yarcombe in East Devon. It is pierced through with a large hole in the centre, with six smaller holes evenly spaced about it. It is labelled a 'Casting Stone', and we are told that a witch would make use of it, in magical workings, by passing things to-and-fro through the holes in a chosen sequence based upon the magical number three and its multiples. Exactly what things were passed through this stone, and what the sequences meant we will most likely never know.

The museum also houses a collection of flint arrowheads which are described as having been passed down within the family of 'Old Hannah' of Moretonhampstead; a town on the edge of Dartmoor. she called them her 'fairy stones' or 'elf shot', and used them for divinations by flicking them one at a time from her thumb and finger into a circle marked out on the ground. From the patterns, directions, and forms of their falling, and with the aid of her spirit familiar Jack, she would make her predictions.

Other tools are of animal origin, such as the 'hoof dippers'; four small 'cups' made from animal hooves. Cecil tells us that witches in the South West will only use 'nature-made' objects to contain their 'lotions, potions and medicinal mixes', and that these examples were used by a witch named 'Old May' from Tiverton.[7]

---

7. The Museum of Witchcraft & Magic, object no.312.

In order to make these magical preparations, Cecil Williamson explains that the morning dew was particularly favoured, and was regarded as being more potent than water drawn from any other source. To gather the dew, small 'basins', six inches wide, and a few inches deep, would be carved into the granite rocks of Dartmoor and Bodmin Moor. The dew would naturally be channelled into these receptacles, from where the witch could collect it for later use.[8]

We have already seen, in the chapter five, that human skulls might be employed to house spirits, or function as 'wish boxes', and that snake vertebrae could be worn to attract powers and spirit forces to the practitioner.

These are just some of the tools said to have been employed by Devonshire witches. Others include such things as candles, pins, thorns, mirrors, switches of twigs, magical staves, stones and animal bones. Via such things might witches convey their magical will, attract spirits and raise power.

For Power & the Sight

A Wise Woman's Charm Bag

From the Honiton district, Cecil Williamson recorded a Devonshire charm bag to be kept by the wise woman and 'Fairy Doctor', and treasured as a source of healing power. To make it, the practitioner will craft a bag of red silk, and within there should be placed certain substances and objects of power. First of these is human hair, then finger nail pairings, and the feet of moles, toads, mice and rats. Numerous wildflower seeds are also to be added, along with bird's feathers, dried herbs and dried root scrapings.[9]

---

8. Howard, Michael. *West Country Witches*, p.112.

9. From one of Cecil Williamson's magical index cards.

A Witches' Herb Gathering Charm 🌿

This charm was said traditionally to be sung by Devonshire witches while gathering herbs for magical purposes. The charm would also be muttered during the preparation of magical herbal concoctions in order to increase their power; [10]

> *'Hail to thee, holy herb,*
> *Growing on the ground,*
> *All on Mount Calvary*
> *First wast thou found.*
> *Thou art good for many sores,*
> *And healeth many a wound;*
> *In the name of St. Jesu!*
> *I take thee from the ground.'*

The muttering of this charm, while concocting drugs or simples, balsams or elixirs, contributes marvelously to their efficacy.

To See Spirits 🌿

To be able to see the 'spirits in the air', collect and mix together the juices of dill, vervain and St John's Wort. Anoint your eyelids with the mixture for three days.[11]

Cure Charms

Blood Stopping 🌿

Of the myriad of traditional cure charms to be found in Devonshire magic, one that seems to have kept the white witches particularly busy is the work of blood stopping; the mysterious art of stopping the flow of blood from an open wound. It is not really surprising that this should

---

10. Hewett, Sarah. *Nummits & Crummits*, p.81.

11. *Ibid*, p.80.

be the case in an area where a significant proportion of the population are engaged in one way or another with agricultural work and its peripheral industries. With all the hazards of farm life, both humans and animals often get into all manner of mishaps, cuts and scrapes.

In such emergencies the white witch or charmer was, and even today still is, called upon to work their influence which, in many cases, they could impart without being in the physical presence of the patient. This meant that a message could be sent out to the practitioner, who could then perform their charm immediately, and in private, causing the bleeding to cease before the doctor or veterinarian could arrive on site and attend to the wound.

When a practitioner did attend to a patient in person, it was an essential precaution to ensure that, on their return home, they did not cross running water; for if they did, the influence if their charm would be negated and the wound would begin to bleed again. If a brook, stream, or river did lay between the patient and the home of the charmer, then a detour, no matter how long, was necessitated.[12] This tradition is obviously cognate with the old belief that spirits, witches and spells could not cross running water.

Most of the old blood stopping procedures employed a spoken charm, which almost always, in various versions, told of Christ's baptism in the River Jordan. The following Devonshire examples are quite typical:

> *Jesus Christ was born in Bethlehem, and was baptised in the river Jordan.*
> *The Child was good,*
> *And the water stood,*
> *And so shall the blood,*
> *In the body of (give the patient's name three times).* '[13]

---

12. St Leger-Gordon, Ruth. *The Witchcraft & Folklore of Dartmoor*, p.169.
13. King, Graham. *The British Book of Spells & Charms*, p.138.

'As Christ was born in Bethlehem and baptised in the river Jordan, He said to the water, "Be still." So shall thy blood cease to flow. In the name of the Father, Son and Holy Ghost. Amen.' [14]

An example recorded in Devonshire dialect;
Jesus wuz borned in Buthlem,
Baptized in tha Jardan, when
Tha watter wuz wild in tha 'ood,
Tha passen wuz jist an' gude,
God spoked and watter stude,
An' zo chell now thy blid.
In the name of the Father, etc. Amen.' [15]

Recorded in the folklore transactions of the Devonshire Association is a different blood stopping charm, in which the operator will press their thumb to their body, in the same part where the patient bleeds, and say:

'And when I passed by thee (give name) and saw thee polluted in thine own blood, I said unto thee, when thou wast in thy blood, Live; yea, I said unto thee when thou wast in thy blood, Live. Then washed I thee with water; yea, I thoroughly washed away thy blood from thee, and I anointed thee with oil. In the name of the Father and of the Son, and of the Holy Ghost. Amen! Amen! Amen!'

To Charm Bleeding at the nose, say nine times with great faith these words, and the bleeding will cease;

'Blood abide in this vein as Christ abideth in the church,
And hide in thee as Christ hideth from himself.' [16]

---

14. Hewett, Sarah. *Nummits & Crummits*, p.68.

15. Hewett, Sarah. *The Peasant Speech of Devon*, p.28.

16. Hewett, Sarah. *Nummits & Crummits*, p.80.

To Charm Warts

Another of the more commonly requested forms of charming for which various methods are employed; including spoken charms, and the use of touch to transfer the warts via some object, which is usually then to be discarded.

The 'transfer item' is often to be buried, so that as it rots, so shall the warts fade. One example calls for the use of prickles harvested from a gooseberry bush; one for each wart. Each prickle is stuck deep into the corresponding wart, and then buried.[17]

A more repellant procedure requires that the head be cut off an eel, which is then used to rub blood onto the warts. The eel head is then buried in the ground so that as it rots the warts will fall off.[18]

Other wart charms require meat, usually bacon, which must be stolen specifically for the purpose. It is commonly touched to the warts and then buried, which at least one example demands should be done at that most useful of folk-magical locations; the crossroads.[19] Another example requires that the meat be used to rub the warts three times from left to right, and that as the meat is buried, a charm should be spoken; *'As you rot, so depart my warts!'* [20]

Other wart charming methods employ the morally questionable act of 'passing on', in which the warts are passed onto an unwitting and innocent random victim. A Devonshire example requires small stones to be gathered from a running stream; one stone for each wart. The stones are tied tightly into a clean white bag, and then thrown into the street. Each wart is washed for

---

17. *Folklore Transactions in the Devonshire Association.*

18. Hewett, Sarah. *Nummits & Crummits*, p.66.

19. *Folklore Transactions in the Devonshire Association.*

20. Hewett, Sarah. *The Peasant Speech of Devon*, p28.

seven successive mornings with strong vinegar. Whoever is unfortunate enough to find and pick up the bag of stones will get the warts.[21]

To Charm Snake Bites 🐍

Adders were once much more common in Devonshire than they are today, although they are around still and bites remain a very occasional hazard for humans and animals walking on the moors, or in the woods. Should a bite occur, a popular remedy was to twist a slender length of hazel into a ring, and place it over the patient's head and around their neck. The folklorist Ruth St. Leger-Gordon wrote in 1965 of applying this remedy, with apparent success, to her black Labrador who had been bitten on the nose.[22]

Sarah Hewett, in 1892, records the same method, but employing a ring of ash, instead of hazel, to be tied about the patient's neck, animal or human, and *'they'll be zartin tu be cured.'* [23]

Other Methods employ spoken charms, of which here are three examples:[24]

The Charmer shall 'strike' the bite three times with nine hazel shots while saying three times the first verse of the 68th psalm; *'let God arise, and then His foes, His enemies, for fear shall run.'*

> *'Adder, adder, adder,*
> *Lay under a stone or down a hole,*
> *He hath done his best wrong,*
> *One-fold, two-fold, three-fold,*
> *In the Name of the Father and the Son,*

---

21. Hewett, Sarah. *Nummits & Crummits*, p.82.

22. St Leger-Gordon, Ruth. *The Witchcraft & Folklore of Dartmoor*, p.184.

23. Hewett, Sarah. *The Peasant Speech of Devon*, p28.

24. Howard, Michael. *West Country Witches*, p.141.

So let this sting passeth away,
From this wretched varmint,
If the Lord so pleases, Amen.'

'Bradely, Bradely, Bradely,
Under the ash, under the ash,
The sting of the Bradely,
The sting of the Bradely,
Go off Bradely,
Go off Bradely,
In the Name of Father, Son
And Holy Ghost,
Amen, amen, amen.'

Spoken Charms for a Thorn Prick 🌿

'Our Saviour Christ was Prick with thorns,
Never Rankled,
Never Fustered,
No more shant thine (give the name of the patient).
Out of the Bone into the flesh,
Out of the flesh into the skin,
Out of the skin into the earth.' [25]

'When Christ was upon middle earth he was prick,
His blood sprung into Heaven.
It shall neither runkle, canker nor rust,
Neither shall thy blood (name of patient),
In the Name of the Father, and of the Son and of the Holy
Ghost,' [26]

'Our dear Lord Jesus Christ was pricked with thorns. His
blood went back to Heaven again, His flesh neither cankered,
rankled, nor festered, neither shall thine, (name of patient).

---

25. King, Graham. *The British Book of Spells & Charms*, p.145.
26. *Ibid*, p.146.

In the name of the Father, Son and Holy Ghost. Amen, Amen, Amen.' [27]

Against Seizures ❦

Here in the south-west, of all trees, the ash perhaps possesses the greatest wealth of magical healing lore. As a charm against fits, a small bundle of ash twigs would be kept in a bag to be worn or carried by the patient. An example of this charm from South Devon, and in a pretty silk bag, is to be found in Scarborough Museum's Clarke collection of charms and amulets, dated 1912.

A cure-charm for epilepsy, provided by a reputed wizard in Exeter, consisted of a powder to be consumed in white wine for the period of one week, and the following magical square inscribed upon paper. It was placed within a bag to be worn about the patient's neck; [28]

Callen Dan Dant
Dan Dant Callen
Dant Callen Dan

A person suffering from fits could perform a cure charm by visiting the parish church at midnight on June the 23rd (St John's Eve), and there walk through each aisle, then crawl three times, from north to south, under the communion table as the clock strikes twelve. [29]

Rings, made from half-crowns or florins, were traditionally used to cure seizures, and their making required the performance of certain rituals. In a Devonshire example, the patient would first beg one penny from thirty people, who must be young and of the opposite sex. These thirty pennies would then

---

27. Hewett, Sarah. *Nummits & Crummits*, p.71.

28. Jones, Kelvin (Ed.) *Folklore & Witchcraft of Devon & Cornwall*, p.4-5.

29. Hewett, Sarah. *The Peasant Speech of Devon*, p28.

be taken to another person who would change them for half-a-crown. This coin then had to be taken to a metal-worker who would be willing to craft it into a ring without payment. The resulting ring had then to be worn constantly by the patient as a charm to ward off fits. A variation of this rite was reported in *The Western Morning News* in 1906. The sufferer, a woman, waited silently in the church porch during the sermon and twelve married men, who had previously been selected for the role, each gave her a penny as they left after the service. A thirteenth man then took the collection of pennies to have them changed for the half-crown coin from which the ring was made.[30]

Against Ague or Fever 🌿
Inscribe the following charm onto parchment, and then bind it over the heart of the patient; *'In the name of St. Exuperus and St. Honorius, fall-fever, spring-fever, quatrain, quintain, ago, super ago, consummatum est.'* As the charm is bound to the patient, the charmer should repeat three Paters and three Aves. It is said that the patient will recover after having worn the charm for nine days.[31]

An anti-ague and fever charm from Marystow, West Devon, is also good against bewitchment;

> *'When Jesus saw the Cross, there to be crucified, Pilate said unto him "What aileth thee? Why shakest thou? Hast thou fever, ague or witchcraft?" Jesus said unto him "I have neither fever, ague or witchcraft, but shake for thy sins." Whosoever carryeth this in his mind or in writing shall have neither fever, ague nor witchcraft. In the name of the Father and of the Son and of the Holy Ghost. Amen and Amen!'* [32]

---

30. King, Graham. *The British Book of Spells & Charms*, p.151-152.

31. Hewett, Sarah. *Nummits & Crummits*, p.82.

32. King, Graham. *The British Book of Spells & Charms*, p.125.

A charm bag against the ague may be made by procuring wood-chips taken from a gallows. These should then be sewn shut within a small bag made from silk and worn over the patient's heart.[33]

In Exeter, a ritual once performed against ague required the sufferer to visit, under the cover of night, the nearest crossroads in order to bury a newly laid egg. This rite had to be performed five times, each time about an hour before the fit was expected. Silence had to be strictly observed throughout, and the patient had to take care not to speak to anyone they might meet on their journey, to or from the crossroads.[34]

Against Toothache 🦷
Whoever keeps the following in the memory, or carries it as a written charm, will never suffer toothache;

> *'As Peter sat weeping on a stone our Saviour passed by and said, 'Peter, why weepest thou?' Peter said unto Him, 'I have got the toothache.' Our Saviour replied, 'Arise and be sound.'* [35]

A similar charm is recorded in the folklore transactions of the Devonshire Association;

> *'Peter stood by the gate of Jerusalem weeping, and the Lord said unto Peter, "Why weepest thou Peter?" an he said "Lord I am sore troubled with the tooth-ache that I know not what to do." The Lord God said "arise Peter and go with God, and I will help thee of tooth-ache." Grant Lord that she that is troubled thou may help them in the name of the Father an of the Son an of the Holy Ghost.'*

---

33. Hewett, Sarah. *Nummits & Crummits*, p.74.

34. Brand, John. *Observations on Popular Antiquities*, p.149.

35. Hewett, Sarah. *Nummits & Crummits*, p.67.

To make a Devonshire toothache remedy, Mix together two quarts of rat's broth. One ounce of camphor. One ounce essence of cloves and take one teaspoonful of the mixture three times a day.[36]

A variation of this recipe calls for a tooth to be taken from a dead rat, which is then to be crush into a powder in a pestle and mortar, and mixed with one ounce of camphor and one ounce of cloves. One teaspoon to be taken three times a day.[37]

A Devonshire ritual to guard against toothache for life was performed by cutting one's toe and finger nails, and wrapping the parings in tissue paper. This small packet was then to be taken out to an ash tree before sunrise, and then inserted carefully into a slit made in the tree's bark.[38]

One could perform another Devonshire anti-toothache ritual by disinterring a human skull, and biting a tooth free from its jaw.[39]

A tooth of a dead person was also carried in Devon, in the left waistcoat pocket, as a charm against toothache.[40] Various other items were also used in Devon as 'pocket charms' against toothache. These include a potato, a lump of sulphur, or a lump of brimstone. As well as warding toothache, these were also considered good preventative charms against rheumatism.[41]

In Scarborough Museum Trust's Clarke Collection of Charms and Amulets, there are two stones which were used in Devon as anti-toothache pocket charms. One is reddish pink in colour, with a white vein of quartz

36. Hewett, Sarah. *Nummits & Crummits*, p.67.

37. Howard, Michael. *West Country Witches*, p.142.

38. Hewett, Sarah. *Nummits & Crummits*, p.75.

39. *Ibid*, p.67.

40. *Ibid*.

41. *Devonshire Association Folklore Transactions*.

running through it. The other stone appears to have been warn smooth by the action of flowing water, and so may possibly have been collected from a stream. The flowing water of streams, and certain stones collected from them, turn up again and again in folk magical rites and charms for healing purposes.

A Charm for Boils 🍃

Arise very early in the morning and go to a thorn bush. On hands and knees, crawl backwards three times around the bush while the dew is still on the grass. Recorded within the folklore transactions of the Devonshire Association.

Against Inflammations 🍃

Also from the same source we find three spoken charms against inflammations. The first is from Marystow;

> *The Queen of Parest is gone into a far country to kill and destroy both men, women, and children, and then her meet our blessed Lord and Saviour Jesus Christ. He said "where are you going thou Queen of Parest?" "I am going into a far country to kill and destroy both men, women, and children". "Thou Queen of Parest turn again: thy evil shall never do harm, in the name of the Father and of the Son, and of the Holy Ghost. Amen.'*

As the second was spoken, we are told that the charmer must pass their hand over the inflammation in the direction of the sun (clockwise) and then down towards the ground;

> *'As our Blessed Virgin Mary was walking over along leading her youngest son by the hand he hang down his head. "Why dew you hang down your hed so low my son?" "my hed doth ake and all my bones." "I fear some ill things you have, I will bless you for ill things". (red ill, wite ill, black ill or blew*

or all other) down to the ground in the name of Lord Jesus Christ. I bless thee (Mention the name of the person) in the name of our Lord Jesus Christ, Amen.'

And the third;

> *'Our Lord Jesus Christ came from the Mount's foot and saw Abraham asleep on the cold ground. Our Lord spoke and said "What liest thou here for?" Abraham spoke and said "It is good to know what I lie here for. I am taken, without blow, aching, burning that I know not what to do." Our Lord Jesus said "Rise up Abraham, rise up from the cold ground – I will make thee safe and sound." In the name of the Father and of the Son, and of the Holy Ghost. Amen.'*

A Devonshire remedy against inflammation called for the inflamed part to be scoured with strong brine, and then washed with plenty of soap and hot water. Much raw beef was then to be consumed for nine days.[42]

Against the Erysipelas 🌿
The Erysipelas, an acute skin infection and rash, is traditionally charmed in Devon by gathering milk from a red cow, and wool taken from beneath the left ear of a black sheep. The wool is dipped into the milk and used to 'strike' the affliction in the direction of the sun, and whilst doing so the following charm is uttered three times; *Now come ye to the Lord of the land, Barney Fine. Barney Gout shall die away under a blackthorn, with red cow's milk and black wool.'* The charmer, when performing this operation, might also hold a bunch of 'may' (hawthorn), and then hang it within the chimney. As the may does wither, so shall the affliction fade.[43]

---

42. Hewett, Sarah. *Nummits & Crummits*, p.72.
43. King, Graham. *The British Book of Spells & Charms*, p.142-143.

To Charm Ringworm or 'Barngun' 🍂

Wool was also employed in rites to charm or bless Ringworm. Three locks of wool would be gathered; one white, one grey, one black, and a basin of clotted cream. Each lock of wool would be dipped into the clotted cream, and then used in succession to apply the cream to the affliction, whilst chanting the following charm in monotone;

> *There were three angels come from the west,*
> *To cure (name or creature) of the barngun,*
> *White barngun, red barngun, black barngun,*
> *Aching, sticking, pricking, barngun,*
> *All sorts of barngun, barngun-būbee, ill will I prove 'e.*
> *I stick thee up on these yer thorn, there thou shalt die,*
> *And never come near'n no more,*
> *In the name of the Father, Son and Holy Ghost. Amen.'*

The cream saturated locks of wool would then be taken to a hawthorn tree, and there hung on its thorns to dry in the wind. This ritual would be repeated five, seven, or nine times according to the severity of the case.[44]

To Cure Itching 🍂

To cure itching in the palm of the hand, a Devonshire rhyme advises one to rub the palm either upon the eye or upon wood; *Rub it on the eye, 'twill go by-and-by; rub it on wood, 'twill sure to come good.'*[45]

To Charm a Burn 🍂

> *Dree angels comed vrom North, East, West,*
> *Wan got vire, wan got ice,*
> *Tha third brot tha Holy Ghost;*

---

44. Hewett, Sarah. *Nummits & Crummits*, p.78.

45. *Ibid*, p.77

Zo, out vire, in vrast!
In the name of the Father, etc.
Amen.' [46]

Another Devonshire variant of this charm comes with the additional information that it would be spoken while the witch passes her hand three times over the burn;

'Three wise men came from the east,
One brought fire, two carried frost.
Out fire! In frost!
In the name of the Father, Son, and Holy Ghost.' [47]

To Charm a Bruise

'Holy chicha! Holy chicha!
This bruise will get well by-and-by.
Up sun high! Down moon low!
This bruise will be quite well very son!
In the Name of the Father, Son, and Holy Ghost.
Amen.' [48]

To Charm Sciatica or 'Boneshave'

Go to a clean river, and there draw water with a pale; dipping it with the direction of the water's flow. Have a pair of iron shears, a large key, and a new table knife. First, dip the knife into the pail of water, draw it back upwards out of the water and then downwards across the hip three times each way. Then dip the key into the water and do the same. Lastly, dip the shears into water, then draw them back out and proceed to 'shear' the hip as though you were shearing wool from it. Make sure to complete the charm by

46. Hewett, Sarah. *The Peasant Speech of Devon*, p.28
47. Hewett, Sarah. *Nummits & Crummits*, p.66.
48. *Ibid*, p.68.

returning the water to the river from which it was drawn. As this is done, the following words are spoken;

'As this water goeth to zay, so flow boneshave away.'[49]

A Charm for Rheumatism

As we have seen with the pocket charms against toothache, potatoes were also used as pocket charms against rheumatism. An early grown kidney potato is dug from the earth and washed. Someone, of the opposite sex to the one who is afflicted, is asked to place it by stealth into a pocket of one of the patient's garments. Once the garment containing the potato has been worn, the patient may transfer it into the pocket of any garment they choose to wear; so that it may always be kept on their person. As the potato begins to shrink and harden, the rheumatism will begin to fade away. It was common among agricultural labourers to carry one in every waistcoat pocket 'until it looks like a small grey stone, and has become quite hard'.[50] I have known an agricultural labourer in Cornwall to continue the practice of keeping a potato in his jacket pocket.

Against Burn-Gout

'Three or four fair maidens came from divers lands crying for burn-gout – aching, smarting, and all kinds of burn-gout – they wentn to the burrow town – there they had brethren three – they went to the salt seas and they never more returned again – he or she shall have their health again. In the name of the Father, and of the Son, and of the Holy Ghost. Amen. So be it.'[51]

---

49. Hewett, Sarah. *Nummits & Crummits*, p. 77-78.
50. *Ibid*, p.78-79.
51. *Devonshire Association Folklore Transactions*.

For Good Sight 🌿

The ingredients for a Devonshire eye strengthening water are given in rhyme; *'Fennel, rose, vervain, celandine and rue, do water make which will the sight renew.'* [52]

To Charm a Sty 🌿

Take a washerwoman's pot stick and a gold wedding ring. First, pass the stick through the ring, then, hold the ring in one hand and 'strike' the afflicted eyelid with the other hand whilst saying;

> *'Pot-ee, pot-ee,*
> *why dist pote me?*
> *To pote the wan out of thine 'ee.'* [53]

To Cure a Sore Throat 🌿

The eighth Psalm is to be read over the patient seven times for three successive mornings:

> *'O Lord, our Lord, how excellent is thy name in all the earth! who hast set thy glory above the heavens. Out of the mouth of babes and sucklings hast thou ordained strength because of thine enemies, that thou mightest still the enemy and the avenger. When I consider thy heavens, the work of thy fingers, the moon and the stars, which thou hast ordained; What is man, that thou art mindful of him? and the son of man, that thou visitest him? For thou hast made him a little lower than the angels, and hast crowned him with glory and honour. Thou madest him to have dominion over the works of thy hands; thou hast put all things under his feet: All sheep and oxen, yea, and the beasts of the field; the fowl of the air, and the fish of the sea, and whatsoever passeth through the paths of the seas. O Lord our Lord, how excellent is thy name in all the earth!'* [54]

---

52. Hewett, Sarah. *Nummits & Crummits*, p.68.

53. *Devonshire Association Folklore Transactions*.

54. Hewett, Sarah. *Nummits & Crummits*, p.76.

To Cure Whooping Cough 🍂

The afflicted child is to be taken into a sheep-fold, and held so that a sheep is able to breathe upon the child's face. One must then watch for a sheep rising to stand; for the child must be set to lie upon the very piece of ground upon which the sheep was lying. This rite must be continued each day for one week.[55]

Another ritual against whooping cough requires an ass to be brought to the door of the house where the afflicted child resides. Into the animal's mouth a slice of new bread is placed, then the child is to be passed three times over and under the animal's body.[56]

Against the Colic 🍂

A strange Devonshire remedy against colic (excessive and unexplained crying), required the mixing of equal quantities of 'elixir of toads' and powdered turkey rhubarb. Half a teaspoonful of this mixture was to be administered to the afflicted child, fasting, for three successive mornings.[57]

Against the King's Evil 🍂

This ritual, performed to create a charm ring against the 'King's Evil' or 'Scrofula'; a swelling of the lymph nodes in the neck caused by tuberculosis, first takes place at the parish church. After the morning service the nearest relative; a male if the patient is a woman, or a female if the patient is a man, will wait on the right-hand side of the church porch, holding a hat, into which people between the ages of sixteen and twenty-one, and again of the opposite sex to the patient, will drop a penny of which thirty are required. The collection of pennies is

---

55. Hewett, Sarah. *The Peasant Speech of Devon*, p.28.

56. Hewett, Sarah. *Nummits & Crummits*, p.79.

57. *Ibid*, p.67.

then to be changed for a silver half-crown. This is to be taken to a metal worker so that the centre of this coin can be cut out, and the outer ring worn as a charm about the neck of the patient. Care must be taken however to keep the centre piece of the coin until the next funeral takes place, when it is to be dropped into the grave just before the coffin is lowered into it.[58]

To Cure Diarrhoea

Place a stale Good-Friday cross-bun into a hot oven until thoroughly dry. This is then kept, so that when it is needed it can be be grated into powder, mixed with cold water and taken as a medicine. Good Friday cross-buns were believed sacred to some degree, and therefor possessed of a special virtue, as the rhyme attests;

> *'When Good-Friday comes, an old woman runs*
> *With one, or two-a-penny hot-cross-buns.*
> *Whose virtue is, if you'll believe what's said,*
> *They'll not grow mouldy like the common bread.'* [59]

Cure Charms and the Dead

There is a long tradition in folk magic of affecting cures via the aid of the dead, and via relics and other items associated with the departed, and such was certainly the case in Devonshire. We have already seen within the anti-toothache charms from the region that teeth kept from someone passed over, or even bitten from the jaw of a disinterred skull, would be employed for their curative influence. Also, within the above ritual against the King's Evil we have seen the use of a newly dug grave. Perhaps, via the principles of sympathetic magic, the influence of death and the dead is being sought within such charms and rites to bring about the 'death' of the malady?

---

58. Hewett, Sarah. *Nummits & Crummits*, p.72.
59. *Ibid*, p.77.

Whilst the hand of the charmer was keenly sought to 'strike' away a multitude of afflictions, the hand of one recently deceased was regarded as possessing the most potent curative touch of all.

Within the 1906 folklore transactions of the Devonshire Association, mention is made of the hand of a dead sailor, recovered from the shipwrecked S.S. Uppingham in 1890, being highly sought to 'strike' the King's Evil.

Rope with which someone had been hanged, either a criminal or a suicide, were also highly sought after and greatly valued for their curative virtues; so much so that they were cut into pieces and sold in Devon by the inch. It is known that these were employed in rites to charm against consumption by 'striking' with the piece of rope.[60]

The reputed power of newly dug graves is illustrated in an intriguing case from Plymouth, in which a man and a woman were observed entering a cemetery at dawn on the 1st of May in 1855. The woman was afflicted with a large growth on her neck and was seen to kneel down beside a newly dug grave from which she took a handful of earth, and rubbed it upon the growth.[61]

Versatile Cures

All manner of ailments could be treated by Devonshire charmers via blessed pieces of cloth, or via lengths of cord or thread in the rite of 'taking the measure'. Strips of cloth or handkerchiefs would be blessed with healing virtue be the charmer, and then bound around the afflicted part of the patient's body; with further spoken cure charms being uttered.

In the rite of taking the measure, the charmer would cut a length of thread or cord to the exact height of the

---

60. King, Graham. *The British Book of Spells & Charms*, p.141.

61. Howard, Michael. *West Country Witches*, p.137.

patient. Again, curative charms would be spoken over it before the charmer took it to some secret place to be buried, or burnt. Via this act, the ailment would fade as the 'measure' rotted in the ground, or as it was consumed by the flames.[62]

Perhaps allied to the Devonshire charmers' use of blessed cloths is the use of a snake skin, formerly to have been found in the collection of the Museum of Witchcraft and Magic. A naturally shed snake skin from Tavistock, which was sadly lost in the terrible flood of 2004, was an example of a charm-skin used within acts of healing. It would be wrapped around the afflicted part, while a charm or chant was spoken, and then left in place for a while before being removed. In the nature of the material we might see the magical intent and symbolism behind the act. Perhaps as the skin is wound around and around the ailment, the healing and regenerative influence of the spirit of the land, the old serpent, is charmed into the affliction, and at its unwinding, the ailment is shed from the body as the snake sheds its skin in renewal.

In the 17th century, rumors of secret witch meetings and strange rituals began to circulate around Faringdon, near Exeter, after a boy witnessed a small group of women at dusk apparently performing a bizarre sacrifice by feeding a baby to a tree. This scene, which caused the boy to flee in fear, was in fact simply the rite of the cleft ash.

In this rite, which varies slightly from version to version, an ailing infant is taken to a young ash tree which is split part way down its middle. The child is then placed into the cleft a certain number of times. At the completion of the rite, the split in the tree must be carefully closed together and bound so that as the cleft grows together again, so will the child grow strong.

---

62. *Ibid*, p.22.

Sarah Hewett wrote in 1892 of the rite of the cleft ash being employed to cure baby boys of hernias. The child's parents would pass him three times through the split in the tree.[63]

In the Museum of Witchcraft and Magic, we find a versatile form of Devonshire cure magic collected by Cecil Williamson. Pin-pricking magic, specifically for curative purposes, is beautifully illustrated in the small figures of a man and a woman, and representations of body parts, collected in Crediton. They are covered over with pin pricks and painted silver. The description card tells us that they are examples of physical aids to the traditional witch's art of distant healing. With each recital of a spoken charm, the figure, which may be made from pastry, wax or clay, is pricked; perhaps to prick at the ailment or to symbolically inject or penetrate the distant target of the working with healing influence. The working of this charm is completed by the figure, or bodily representation, being coated with egg-white, varnish or paint.

The act of sticking, pinning, threading and impaling is central to numerous magical operations, and is most often associated in popular thought with the magic of cursing, this is obviously not always the case. Pins, nails and thorns are part of the stock items of the folk-magician's working tools. The piercing or sticking of a symbolic item in traditional magic might be seen as 'pinning down' or 'fixing' one's will and intent upon the target of the magical working. The 'phallic' form of the penetrating pin, nail, or thorn, is cognate also with the 'creative act' and with fertility; giving life unto the magician's will and unto the spell or charm. Thus, it is a method employable for all manner of magical purposes.

Another versatile method of magic employed in Devon and the West Country, although exclusively used to be rid

---

63. Hewett, Sarah. *The Peasant Speech of Devon*, p.27.

of things, is the 'get lost box'. These were prepared by wise women and white witches to contain something that their client wished to be rid of, often an ailment or bodily complaint of some sort. Sometimes these boxes might contain symbolic items relating to that which was to be banished, or perhaps knots in a string that have been touched to the affliction. An example from Plymouth is to be found in the Museum of Witchcraft and Magic, fashioned to resemble a parcel by a wise woman who worked the morally questionable act of 'passing on magic'. What appears to the passer-by to be a dropped and unaddressed parcel will contain some unwanted nasty thing, such as warts or corns. If someone opens the package, they will become afflicted with whatever it was the original patient wished to be rid of.

Curse Magic

Image Magic 🜨
That which most comes to mind, when mention is made of a witch's curse magic, is perhaps the use of image magic; via the use of the witch's 'poppet', or 'mommet'. These constructions, not always intended for malefic purposes, are of course made to represent the actual target of the magical operation, and will help convey the witch's will to their 'victim'; for any action enacted upon the image is intended to befall the person it represents. This is an ancient and widespread method of magic, and it is therefore not surprising to find examples of its use in Devonshire also.

In the Dartmoor village of Widecombe, a woman was known to have employed image magic in order to place curses upon those who displeased her. To cause her neighbor to suffer aches and cramp, she stuck pins and needles into a doll. On another occasion, she fashioned a likeness of someone out of dough, and placed the image upon her hearth and around it laid a circle of gun powder. As she ignited the powder, she willed the person represented to be struck with a fever leading to death.[64]

A number of intriguing examples of image magic from the region, which reveal more about this method, can be viewed today in the collection housed in Museum of Witchcraft and Magic.

A collection of beeswax poppets is displayed along with a beautifully made wooden coffin-box, which Cecil Williamson tells us belonged to a wealthy witch and clairvoyant medium from Exeter who went by the name Madam de la Cour. When a poppet was to be used, herbs and written charms would be enclosed and sealed within a hollow in its back, along with items such as nail parings and hair procured somehow from the intended victim of the curse, to help magically link and identify them with the image. Madam de la Cour would then shut the curse poppet within the coffin-box, and there leave it to work its ill-influence.

Another poppet in the collection was made to represent a well-to-do lady from Exmouth, who it seems possessed a 'mean and spiteful nature'. To assist in the magical identification of this image with the woman it represents, it was created using material cut from her own clothing; stolen from her wardrobe. The blade of an old stiletto knife, which was also taken from the woman's home, is inserted into one of the poppet's eyes and driven, with some force, right through its face.

Another of the museum's examples of image magic was made to represent only the victim's head and face, again utilizing material taken from their clothing. It is from Paignton and dated 1956. Cecil Williamson, writing about this artefact, explains; 'Tittle-tattle is the curse of every village and hamlet in the UK. Well, this is how they deal with scandal-mongers in the south west. Items won

---

64. Howard, Michael. *West Country Witches*, p.151.

secretly from Miss Wagging Tongue are fashioned into a face and a nice sharp needle or pin stuck through that false tongue.' [65]

The careful construction of a poppet will perhaps always remain a favorite method of image magic, however, with the invention of the camera, the photographic image inevitably became an important part of the modern witch's arsenal. Being formed by light bouncing from the body of the magical target, the photograph is already, in magical thought, innately 'linked' with the one it depicts. In the collection of the Museum of Witchcraft and Magic, we find photographs being employed magically, alongside the more traditional poppets of wax and clay. One example of photographic curse magic from Exeter depicts a woman, and the edges of the photograph have been carefully and deliberately singed. In working the curse, the witch allowed the edges of the image to burn slowly whilst employing her breath to blow the smoldering convergence of her ill-will towards her victim. One can imagine the potency of an act of magic combining the elements of image, focus, fire and breath. Cecil Williamson reveals this to have been a case of 'leave my husband alone' magic.

It would seem that the inclusion of things intimate to the target of a magical working; their hair cuttings, nail parings, personal clothing etc. are most crucial to forming an actual magical link, and that the created image or poppet is mostly to aid the focus and concentration of the witch. Some examples of curse magic from the region however do away with the image, and make use only of materials intimate to the victim.

The Curse Stick 🜨

On one of Cecil Williamson's magical index cards, housed in the archives of the Museum of Witchcraft

---

65. Museum of Witchcraft & Magic, object no.223.

and Magic, is recorded a 'Killing Charm' from Totness. To work this charm the witch, or their client, would have to gather such things as bread crusts from the victim's table, hair from their comb, and strips of material torn from unwashed undergarments. These things would then be bound together in a special paste made with herbs and glutinous flour. The whole sticky mass is then bound around the middle of a specially prepared stick with string, and at each end of this stick is tied a string terminating in a holed flint stone, or hagstone. This 'curse stick' is then to be taken to a large, solitary old oak tree, around which lengthy dances and incantations are made. At the climax of this rite, the curse stick is to be flung high into the tree where the hagstone-weighted strings will entangle themselves around its branches, and there the thing will be 'left to the forces of nature.'

The Herring-Bone Death Charm 🍂

This Devonshire curse ensures intimacy with its victim by their unwitting close contact with the charm itself. It is enacted by sewing a long and thin herring bone into a garment which the victim will be wear next to their skin. As the bone dries up and withers, so it is intended that the victim of the curse will pine away and die.[66]

Evil in the Air 🍂

In folk-magical belief we might find that spells and spirits, whether benevolent or malevolent in nature, are thought to travel through the air, often to enter the home via the chimney. Such a belief is perhaps evidenced by the tradition of placing or hanging protective charms and counter curses within the chimney, above the hearth-fire. It would seem also to be the case that protective charms were sometimes hidden in the highest place within the home or barn, perhaps by being placed upon a roof beam.

---

66. Hewett, Sarah. *Nummits & Crummits*, p.82.

This could be to place all that lay beneath the charm under its protection, but again it may be linked to a belief in air travelling spirits. The use of feathers and other bird parts in folk magic might also hint at such beliefs, and there are a number of intriguing examples house in the Museum of Witchcraft and Magic's collection.

For example, one will find a beautiful blue and white plate holding a bird's nest which contains four bird skulls, discovered in 1968 hidden in a sealed off roof space in an old cottage in Noss Mayo, South-West Devon. The old description card describes this artefact as a cursing charm intended to harm four people, represented by the skulls, whilst the nest represents their home, and the blue and white plate represents the sky and clouds. Others however have suggested that, due to its placement, this may instead have been a protective charm as many examples are discovered in roof spaces.

Another bird related artefact in the collection, which would appear undoubtedly to be a curse charm, is a rather grizzly looking item. A little sparrow is entombed in wax within a red shoe. We are told that it was created for a client, as the result of hate and jealousy, by a charmer known as 'Black Dorris' from Union Street in Plymouth. This artefact particularly horrified me upon my first visit to the museum with my parents. Fortunately, however, the bird doesn't appear to have been a living one when it went into the shoe; because on closer inspection I realised it has the glass eyes of a taxidermy specimen.

Magical Protection & Defense

Protective Hagstone Charms 🍃

The hagstone; a stone, usually of flint, possessing a natural portal opened by the action of water, is one of the most common and ancient protective amulets to be found within traditional folk magic. Almost always, when such stones are employed for amuletic purposes, they are threaded through with such things as cord, string, leather thongs and sometimes metal wire. Here, in addition to the natural amuletic properties of the holed stone, we also encounter thread and knot magic. Threads, cords and knots have a long use within magic to contain and convey intent, as well as to trap and confuse spirits, and, in some cases, to keep them occupied or entertained.

Perhaps in the threading of cord or string through the magical holed stone, tying in it a knot to form a loop, we find a safeguarding against dangerous otherworld forces. Alternatively, we might see such a practice as calling upon and manifesting the aid of the spirit world, for in knot magic, intent is the key. Also, the combination of cord and hole could be reminiscent, or symbolic, of the 'creative act'; being in magical thinking a concept deeply associated with potency and the manifestation of intent, as well of course as the nullification of its opposite; destructive and evil force.

In the Museum of Witchcraft and Magic, we find a hag stone charm, prepared by a witch in Bridestowe, West Devon. Eight hag stones are threaded onto a string tied with five knots. Within this charm, which was hung up in a stable, hagstones, thread and knot magic combine to protect horses from being night ridden by pixies.

A number of interesting hagstone charms from Devonshire are held in the Scarborough Museums Trust's collection of charms and amulets. One of these consists of a single hagstone, threaded onto knotted twine, and is labelled a 'Marestane'. It was prepared and sold by an Exmouth wise woman in 1910 to be hung on a bedstead to ward off nightmares. The description card explains that the charm does this by keeping away 'Mara', the evil spirit who disturbs our slumbers.

Hagstones are also sometimes threaded together with other items, and in the same collection we find an interesting charm which consists of three hagstones, and part of the pelvic bone of a sheep with a natural hole in it, all threaded together on string. This charm was also prepared and sold by an Exmouth wise woman, perhaps the same one, around 1910, for the purpose of keeping witches away.

Another of the collection's hagstone charms is threaded together with an old key; bringing with it the traditional protective and potent virtues of iron. This charm was collected in 1913 and was hung in a cottage in Devonshire, also as a protection against witchcraft.

A particularly beautiful hagstone charm, housed in the Museum of Witchcraft and Magic, was made by Nick Westmancoat. It is in the form of a rope hand-pull for hauling a boat ashore, and is intricately woven to encase a hagstone in its end. In Devon, a boat's hauling rope should be passed through a hagstone to protect it from evil spirits. Hagstones would also be nailed or tied within the bows of a boat to protect it from being 'witched'.[67]

Pricked Hearts 🦋

Hearts from various animals have a long use within witchery and folk magic as a form of counter-cursing, in which the ill-intent of the malevolent practitioner is lifted from their victim and redirected upon them, so that they will suffer the effects of their own maleficia. Where an animal had died, and an ill-wisher was suspected of causing the death by magical means, the animal's owner was often directed to remove the heart from the animal's carcass, to stick it with such things as pins, thorns and nails, and to cause the heart to burn, often by hanging it within the chimney over the fire. In so doing, it was believed that the ill-wisher would be tormented, and their power nullified, or that they might even be killed.

The Clarke collection in Scarborough includes an unusual example of a pricked heart charm, in the form

---

67. Museum of Witchcraft & Magic, description card for object no.2042.

of a seagull's heart, stuck with four pins. It was collected from South Devon in 1910 and was used to reverse a curse. Through the top of the heart is tied a loop of thread, possibly to allow it to be hung up somewhere in the cottage. In the same collection we also find a sheep's heart, stuck full with nails and pins and also used in South Devon as a charm to lift the influence of witchcraft.

Michael Howard writes of a Devonshire counter curse which required one to obtain a sheep's heart and stick it full of pins whilst saying *'May each pin thus stuck in this poor heart, in hers to go who hurts me till she departs.'* The pin-stuck heart must then be hung within the chimney and left there to work its influence upon the evildoer. A Devon woman, suffering from breast cancer, was scheduled in 1905 to have the growth surgically removed in Tiverton Hospital. However, she was told by a wise-woman that her condition had been caused by ill wishing and that she could cure herself by performing this spell. The woman did as she was advised and would later find that she no longer required the operation as her tumor had vanished. Shortly after placing the heart in her chimney, one of the woman's neighbours suddenly became ill and grew weaker and weaker until she died. It was believed then that she had been the woman's ill-wisher, and that as she faded and died so too did the woman's breast cancer.[68]

The Museum of Witchcraft and Magic houses a heart, believed to be that of a dog, which is stuck with nine pins and was recovered from the pathway leading to Cecil Williamson's house. He concluded that it was a curse fueled by the Cornish being not too keen on 'come ins', and he set about reversing its influence by the use of magic mirrors. However, given the traditional use of the pin stuck heart, it has been suggested that this heart may have been put in place as a counter-curse by someone who feared that Cecil might have put a curse on them.

---

68. Howard, Michael. *West Country Witches*, p.161-162.

Frog & Toad Counter-Curses ✤

There seems always to have been an affinity amongst witches with frogs, and toads in particular, and there are, of course, many cases of witches keeping and cosseting their amphibian friends as treasured familiars and assistants to their magical workings. It is perhaps for this reason that these poor creatures have often suffered at the hand of those seeking to work against the suspected witch. A rather cruel ritual to lift the influence of a 'black witch' is recorded from Chittlehamholt, North Devon, in the 1820s, and was known as 'flying the witch'. It involved a seesaw being made by balancing a plank of wood upon a log and placing a toad upon one end of the plank. The other end was stuck a heavy blow, thus sending the poor creature flying through the air, by which the curse was believed to have been lifted and returned upon the witch.[69]

Sarah Hewett records an intriguing ritual to 'Destroy the Power of a Witch'. Thorns from a holy thorn bush, new pins and three small-necked stone jars are gathered, along with three frog livers and three toad hearts. The frog livers are first stuck full with pins, and the toad hearts stuck full with thorns, and one of each is put into the three stone jars. Three different churchyards are then visited, and in each, one of the stone jars is to be buried in the churchyard path; seven inches from the surface and seven feet from the porch. While burying each jar the Lord's prayer should be repeated backwards. As the pin-stuck livers and thorn-stuck hearts rot away, so will the witch's power fade. It is said that no witch can have any power over whoever who performs this rite.[70]

Interestingly, it appears that in 1875 the Rev. W.T. Wellacott of Bradworthy not only uncovered evidence of this rite, or one closely relating to it, having been

---

69. Howard, Michael. *West Country Witches*, p.162-163.

70. Hewett, Sarah. *Nummits & Crummits*, p.74.

performed, but he demonstrated knowledge of the procedure. Writing to the Western Morning News, he explained that a small glazed and corked jar had been found buried in the churchyard path while preparing it for fresh gravel, about three inches below the surface, and about eight feet from the porch. Inside it was found to contain a number of pins and thorns. The Reverend also explained that he believed the jar to have been buried in his churchyard as part of a ritual to destroy the power of a witch, and that there must be two other jars buried in two other churchyards, for three such burials were required for the rite to be successful.[71]

Protection by Iron 🌿

Being heavily associated with fire, the magic of the forge, and martial virtue; iron, and those objects crafted from it, has a long established usage in the magic of spiritual protection and defense. Like running water, it was believed that witches, evil spirits and spells could not cross iron, hence perhaps the popularity of the horseshoe on or above the door; that most widespread and perhaps often unwitting form of folk magic enacted still today.

In Devon, the affixing of the horseshoe 'to frustrate the power of the black witch', was accompanied with ritual. A used horseshoe would be nailed above the door, points upwards. As the nails were being hammered in place, one would chant the following in monotone;

> *'So as the fire do melt the wax*
> *And wind blows smoke away*
> *So in the presence of the Lord*
> *The wicked shall decay,*
> *The wicked shall decay.*
> *Amen'* [72]

---

71. Howard, Michael. *West Country Witches*, p.165.
72. Hewett, Sarah. *Nummits & Crummits*, p.68.

A Devonshire talisman for protection from enemies, and to counteract the power of the evil eye, requires a disk of cast iron and the preparation of an incense called 'Burnt Spirits of Mars'. This is made by mixing together red saunders (red sandalwood), frankincense and red pepper. Upon the night of the full moon, the iron disk is to be carefully engraved with the following sign;

Once inscribed, the disk is then to be fumigated with the Burnt Spirits of Mars incense, and then suspended around the neck of the one to be protected.

Whilst iron is perhaps the ideal material for this talisman, we are advised that it may be made from any material, in any form, and in any size. For example, the characters of the talisman could be inscribed on the inside of a gold ring. In whatever form this talisman is made, it is most important that it be made on the night of the full moon, and that the correct incense is used before it is worn.[73]

Maiden nails, being newly forged nails that have not yet been used for any purpose and that have not been allowed to touch the ground, are highly prized within traditional magic. The folklore transactions of the Devonshire Association for 1880 record their use to render a witch powerless. The maiden nails must be procured from a smith and taken to the door of the witch's home. There, drive the nails deep into the witch's threshold. When the witch crosses over the nails, their power will be drained.

---

73. *Ibid*, p.73-74.

Alternatively, one could watch the witch carefully while out walking. Drive a maiden nail into one of the witch's footprints, made by their left foot, for the same result.

Protective Written Charms 🐌

The word '*Abracadabra*' inscribed upon parchment, in the form of an inverted triangle and in such a manner that it diminishes from the full word down to a single letter, was an old favourite amongst the white witches, and was often prescribed to clients wishing to be rid of such things as illness and bewitchment. These inscribed parchments would most often be worn by the patient, and as the word itself diminishes, so it was believed the patient's affliction would be influenced to diminish also.

Certainly, this charm was employed in Devonshire, and there is record of the Abracadabra charm, written on parchment and enclosed within a black silk bag, being given by an Exeter white witch to a client. It was to be worn about the neck and its purpose was to provide protection 'gainst the dominion of the grey witch, pixies, evil spirits and the powers of darkness.' Its cost was one guinea, and the white witch's client was advised that it should never be removed, and that if it were ever allowed to fall to the ground then its power would be lost and a new charm would have to be prepared to replace it.[74]

```
A B R A C A D A B R A
A B R A C A D A B R
A B R A C A D A B
A B R A C A D A
A B R A C A D
A B R A C A
A B R A C
A B R A
A B R
A B
A
```

74. Hewett, Sarah. *Nummits & Crummits*, p.73.

Crossing Over Fire 🥀

Recorded in 1897, from the North Devon parish of Chittlehamholt is a ritual to be enacted in order to lift the influence of having been 'overlooked' by a witch. By whatever means, it is required that entry be gained into the home of the witch so that three burning sticks may be taken from the hearth, and these must then be placed upon the ground. The one who is suffering from having been overlooked must then walk over the burning sticks three times before the fire is extinguished with water, thus presumably extinguishing the influence of the witch.[75]

Protective Herb Charms 🥀

In Devonshire, St John's Wort (*Hypericum perforatum*) is known also as Devil's Flight. To create a charm from the region to 'dispel vapours, and to drive away evil spirits' gather the herb on St John's Day (June the 24th) or on a Friday. Ensure that the herb is dried thoroughly and place it within a closely-covered jar. Attach this with cords or string so that it may be hung in a window to protect the house from thunderbolts, storms, fire, and evil spirits.[76]

Other plants traditionally used in Devon for protective purposes include Elder (*Sambucus nigra*), which if planted beside a house will guard against evil influences. Also regarded as potent protectors against evil are garlic (*Allium sativum*), vervain (*Verbena*) and navalwort or pennywort (*Umbilicus rupestris*).[77]

Against Vermin 🥀

To keep fleas, beetles, earwigs or 'vermin' of any sort out of the house, one must take note of where one's

---

75. King, Graham. *The British Book of Spells & Charms*, p.209.

76. Hewett, Sarah. *Nummits & Crummits*, p.75.

77. Farquharson-Coe, A. *Devon's Witchcraft*, p.32.

right foot is standing at the very moment one first hears the cuckoo in Spring. Some earth must be taken from this very spot and taken home to be sprinkled across the threshold of one's door. Tell no one of your actions and no unwelcome critters will be able to cross it.[78]

Against Drowning ❧

The 'wish bone', or 'merrythought', kept aside from the remains of various birds consumed at the dinner table, is of course widely associated with good luck and the making of wishes. However, they were also seen to possess protective virtues; for in Scarborough Museum's Clarke collection, there is an example of one such bone accompanied by a description which tells us that wishbones or merrythoughts were carried by sailors in Devonshire as charms against drowning.

A Protective Prayer-Charm ❧

To bring protection against all thieves and enemies, the following prayer-charm is to be said daily at sunrise;

> *'In the power of God, I walk on my way,*
> *In the meekness of Christ, what thieves soe'er I meet,*
> *The Holy Ghost to-day shall me keep.*
> *Whether I sit, stand, walk or sleep,*
> *The shining of the sun,*
> *Also the brightness of his beams, shall me help.*
> *The faith of Isaac to-day shall me lead;*
> *The sufferings of Jacob to-day be my speed.*
> *The devotion of the holy Lamb thieves shall let,*
> *The strength of Jesus's passion them beset,*
> *The dread of death hold thieves low,*
> *The wisdom of Solomon cause their overthrow.*
> *The sufferings of Jacob set them in hold,*
> *The chastity of Daniel let what they would.*

---

78. Hewett, Sarah. *Nummits & Crummits*, p.75.

The speech of Isaac their speech shall spill,
The languishing faith of Jerom let them of their will.
The flaming fires of hell to hit them I bequeath,
The deepness of the deep sea, their hearts to grieve.
The help of Heaven cause thieves to stand,
He that made sun and moon bind them with his hand.
So sure as St. Bartholomew bound the fiend,
With the hair of his beard.
With these three sacred names of God known and unknown,
Miser, Sue, Tetragrammaton, Christ Jesus! Amen.' [79]

Love Charms

Plant Charms for Love 🌿

Gather and dry some St John's Wort. On the evening on the July full moon, grind the flowers and leaves in a pestle and mortar into a fine powder. Place this powder into a silken bag, and whoever wears this charm about their neck will be successful in all matters of love. By this charm they shall also be 'cured of the vapours and all mental afflictions.' [80]

The Willow, being of watery and lunar virtue, is deeply associated in the magical mind with all matters of the heart, and in the Museum of Witchcraft and Magic we find three , 195s tied into a slender willow branch. It was recovered from a streamside tree in Tavistock. Its description card tells us that the west country the witch might direct a lovelorn client to a willow tree, growing beside a river, and there to tie knots in a trailing branch end followed by a love meditation and a spoken charm. [81]

---

79. Hewett, Sarah. *Nummits & Crummits*, p.79-80.

80. *Ibid*, p.75.

81. Museum of Witchcraft & Magic, description card for object no.294

Gather the root of mandrake, and the seeds of poppy, to be dried and ground into a fine powder. Take the body of a green frog and place it in an ant hill. When enough time has passed to allow the ants to consume the flesh, retrieve the frog bones and grind these also into a fine powder, which is then to be mixed with the powder of mandrake and poppy. This mixture is made into cakes, formed into the shape of a breast, and crumbled secretly into the food of the one you desire.[82]

Good Fortune

The Three Bees Charm 🐝

Among the Museum of Witchcraft and Magic's collection of West Country charms, we find a little blue leather drawstring pouch with its three little bees, once concealed within. We are told that this is a traditional and widely used Devonshire charm, and that this particular example was recovered in 1949 from Dawlish.

The purpose of the three bees charm, which would be hung up in the best room in the house, is to bring health, happiness and good fortune.

The meaning behind the charm might be found within the traditional significance of bees in occult thinking; for they are symbols of the soul, productivity, the sun, and the taking up of nourishment from the dew-fall of divine nectar. This then is a very fitting charm to encourage the blessings of the spiritual world, and that which feeds the soul. The description card for this artefact also gives some sound advice regarding witch charms, for we are warned that whilst the draw string pouch variety are safe enough for a peep inside, those that are sealed shut must never be opened and are best left well alone.

---

82. Howard, Michael. *West Country Witches*, p.143.

Lucky Stones ❦

A variety of stones are traditionally carried for such purposes as good fortune, good luck and protection, and are usually selected for some special quality in their form or appearance. Naturally holed stones are of course most sought after, but crystalline stones of quartz, found brought to the surface in a ploughed field perhaps, are also valued, as are stones with veins of quartz; especially if they happen to form the shape of the cross. Stones pinkish or red in colour are also desirable. In Devonshire, whilst the white witches are out on their country walks, they will keep a keen eye out for any lucky stones that they can later bless and incorporate into the charms supplied to their clients.[83]

Moon Customs for Good Fortune ❦

One can ensure good luck, at the time of the new moon, by means of a simple ritual. Go outside with your purse and look to the new moon. Turn the purse three times round the pocket whilst curtseying and saying; *'Welcome, new moon! Welcome, new moon!'* [84]

The folklore transactions of the Devonshire Association record the same ritual, as well as the Devon tradition that it is unlucky to see the new moon through glass. Should this happen, the situation can be remedied by going outside and looking at the new moon over one's right shoulder.

Lucky Coal ❦

Like pennies and pins, finding a piece of coal is regarded as a fortunate event. To ensure good luck, one Devon tradition advises one to spit upon the piece of coal before throwing it over the right shoulder. Another tradition tells us that good luck will be attracted by keeping a small piece of coal in the purse.[85]

---

83. *Ibid*, p.21.

84. Hewett, Sarah. *The Peasant Speech of Devon*, p.72.

85. *Folklore Transactions in the Devonshire Association*.

Coal washed up by the sea is regarded as particularly lucky. Whist visiting the Museum of Witchcraft and Magic, a fisherman from South Devon told staff there that his family had a tradition of carrying a piece of sea coal aboard their fishing boats to ensure good fortune.

The most fortunate coal however is said to be that found buried beneath the roots of a mugwort plant (*Artemisia vulgaris*) or plantain (*Plantago major*) on midsummer's eve. It can then be worn or carried as a potent charm, and will protect from such things as plague, carbuncle, lightening, the quartan ague, and burning.[86]

A Written Charm for Success 🌿

Inscribe this charm upon virgin parchment and sew it shut within a round silken bag. Whoever wears this charm continuously over their heart will be successful in all undertakings, including matters of love.[87]

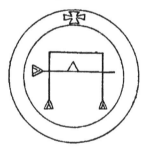

Gambler's Luck 🌿

In addition to its uses within curative magic, the hempen rope with which a person has been hanged was used in Devon to secure luck during games of chance. A section of the rope would be worn about the neck on a silken cord during such pursuits.[88]

---

86. *Folklore Transactions in the Devonshire Association.*

87. Hewett, Sarah. *Nummits & Crummits*, p.74.

88. *Ibid*, p.65.

To Restore Lost Money

The following bizarre incantation was employed by a Devonshire white witch to restore lost sums of money to their clients;

> *'Flibberty, gibberty, flasky flum,*
> *Calafac, tarada, lara, wagra wum.*
> *Hooky, maroosky, whatever's the sum,*
> *Heigho! Presto! Money come!*
> *In the name of the Father, the Holy Ghost, and Son.*
> *Amen! Amen!'* [89]

For All Purposes

The Witch's Swing

We have heard of Cecil Williamson's encounter with a woman, whilst at his boarding school in Buckinghamshire, who taught him how to use a swing and a fire in order to put a curse on his school bully. He wrote of a slight variation of this method to accompany an image of a witch using a swing, once displayed in his museum. Instead of a fire, an image or representation of the target of the spell is placed on the ground beneath the swing. We also learn that this is a versatile form of magic making, because it can be used to curse or to bless;

'When a Devon or Cornish witch wishes to hex a thing or person, she often makes use of her swing – the principle is simple: set up a swing from the branch of a tree in a chosen pulse spot location, under the swing place the object or the image of the subject to be hexed or blessed. Then start swinging to and fro in rhythm to the chanted incantations, passing backwards and forwards over the objects on the ground directly beneath the swing's path. This form of magic making

---

89. *Ibid*, p.72.

is of Celtic origin and is confined to the western areas of England.' [90]

The 'Pixy Pyramid' 🍃

Wind, smoke, fire and direction were important tools within Cecil's magical work, and he wrote about their use on numerous occasions. In the garden of his home, in the Devon village of Witheridge, was a strange construction which appears to have been a magical device utilizing all four of these tools. Cecil referred to this contraption, jokingly, as his 'pixy pyramid'.[91] A stepped square 'pyramid' base of concrete was topped with a large metal directional 'compass', complete with a rotating pointer. Above this was a tripod from which a metal fire basket was hung on chains. It appears that, in magical workings, Cecil would position the directional pointer in the direction of the target of his will, and would light a fire above this in the basket, allowing the wind to carry his magical influence within the rising smoke.[92]

Mirror Magic 🍃

Another of Cecil Williamson's favourite magical tools was the mirror; both of the silvered kind, and of the dark kind. The normal silvered kind, it appears, was used for protective purposes; to reflect back curses, trouble and ill-intent upon wrongdoers. They were also used to contact and communicate with spirits and the spirit world. Most favored for this kind its seems are the 'witch mirrors' carved in the form of a squatting witch-like figure, complete with pointed hat. Numerous examples are known. There is a fine example on display in the Museum of Witchcraft and Magic, and the witch Doreen Valiente possessed one also. I

---

90. Museum of Witchcraft & Magic, object no.404.

91. Howard, Michael. *West Country Witches*, p.111.

92. King, Graham. 'Cecil Williamson & the Witchcraft Museum', *The Cauldron* no.136 p.23

was lucky enough to have acquired an example myself, and certainly find it an interesting item to work with magically. For contacting the spirit world, Cecil suggested that the mirror should be positioned so that it is pointing just over one's shoulder. One should then gaze into the mirror for no less than half an hour to get results. Eventually, the spirits would make themselves known.[93]

The dark mirror, being of framed clear glass which has been coated on the reverse with multiple layers of black paint, also has its uses for conjuring and communicating with spirits; particularly those of the dead, however, Cecil Williamson had a particularly potent magical use for the dark mirror which could be employed to influence another. This involved the mirror being set up with a candle in front of it, and required an item or substance to aid the witch in making a magical link with the target of their working. A photograph of the person concerned could be placed beneath the candle for example, or something taken from their home placed between it and the mirror. Cecil preferred to collect a spider's web from somewhere in his home, asking and thanking the spider, and draping it over his dark mirror. He chose a spider's webs because no matter how immaculate and house-proud a person professes to be, there will always be a spider's web somewhere in their home.

With the mirror, contact item and candle set up, the candle is lit and a pin is to be pushed through it whilst concentrating on the desired result of the working. As the candle burns, one must then gaze deeply into the dark mirror; focusing intently on the situation and 'seeing' the desired result taking effect. This deep magical focus must be maintained until the flame has reached the pin and caused it to fall from the candle.[94]

93. Patterson, Steve. *Cecil Williamson's Book of Witchcraft*, p.256-257.

94. Morgan, Levannah. 'Mirror, Moon & Tides', *Hands of Apostacy*, p.223.
Also; Patterson, Steve. *Cecil Williamson's Book of Witchcraft*, p.257.

Charms for Animals

Two witch-prepared animal skulls from Devon may be found today in the Museum of Witchcraft and Magic. One is a skull spirit house; revealing that such a thing can function as a charm by having a spirit, or force, conjured into it in order to perform a specific magical task, or to occupy spirits that might otherwise become troublesome. In this case, a horse skull, which looks to be that of a mare, was hung in a barn, on the high cross-beam, of a Drewsteignton farm in 1927. Its purpose was to occupy the nightmare riding spirits.

The second skull, a pig's skull with a brass heart symbol affixed to its forehead, is a good example of the general protective uses to which a charmed and spirit filled skull could be put. The heart sign, being a protective and fortunate motif in itself, often featured in horse-brasses, which are of course items with their own tradition of magical protective use. The museum's pig skull was prepared and empowered by a witch in the 1940s to function as a general protective charm for a farm in the Cullompton area.

Also within the Museum of Witchcraft and Magic we find a charm in which the protective properties of bone and iron have been brought together to form a magical 'Horse Guard', created by a Devon witch using a section of cow bone fastened through by an iron chain. It was hung on a stable door to protect the horses from thieves.

As well as the traditional magically protective and defensive properties of iron, the binding and fastening nature of the chain might serve to aid the keeping of the horses safe from theft. There might also be an element of calling upon the aid of the spirit world in the threading of the chain through the bone, for as we have seen, threading through, or the passing of something through a hole, from one side to another, to form a loop, is traditionally employed in the magical use of hagstones, and of course there is the very ancient use of protective amuletic beads.

Rowan, or 'care' as it is known in the West Country was widely used for its reputed powers not only to protect humans from bewitchment, but particularly for the protection and wellbeing of cattle and horses. Animals suffering any affliction would be wreathed with care to 'stop them getting worse.' [95]

When the witch and author Michael Howard lived in Somerset in the early 1960s, he was able to observe that farmers there were still keen to ward off witches and fairies by nailing care branches above the doors of their barns and cowsheds. Interestingly, this was always done on May's Eve and at Hallowe'en. He also discovered that the practice still continues on farms in some of the more remote parts of Somerset and Devon.[96]

In 1908, a cure charm for 'kebbit', a cracked heel in a bullock, was recorded in Devon. One had to wait for the afflicted animal to lay down, and then watch very carefully when he stands up again; taking notice of the very spot of turf where he first places his bad foot. One then had to cut out this piece of turf in the shape of a hoof and then replace it again up-side-down.[97]

Foot and Mouth disease, or the 'murrion' as it was known, never used to cause the blind panic with which people have reacted to it in recent times, and this relatively mild condition was treated with various remedies and charms. In 1910, a farmer, living between Tavistock and Plymouth, consulted a white witch when his cattle became afflicted, and was told to perform a peculiar ritual. First, he had to draw a circle on the ground somewhere on

---

95. King, Graham. *The British Book of Spells & Charms*, p.188.

96. Howard, Michael. *West Country Witches*, 2010, p.169.

97. King, Graham. *The British Book of Spells & Charms*, p.187.

his land, and take a white cockerel. The bird had to be thrown up in the air so that it would land in the circle whereupon it would be found, mysteriously, to be dead. The disease would then begin to leave the farmer's herd.

After performing the rite, the farmer was amazed to find that the cockerel, which had been alive and perfectly healthy when he threw it up in the air, was indeed already dead when it hit the ground within the circle. Just as the white witch had said, the farmer's cattle recovered; their affliction having been taken away with the life of the white cockerel.[98]

In the Museum of Witchcraft and Magic, there has long been on display an intriguing wand, with one end split in such a way that it may hold an egg, and the other end sharpened into a point. It was used by a Betty Coles in the Umberleigh area of North Devon in order to combat diseases in chickens in the 1920s. Cecil Williamson writes beautifully of this wand and the magical significance of the egg;

'The spirit force hand, in which it holds the egg of life, the great ovum. The country witch of the western shires makes use of naturally found things for her magic-making – eggs of all sorts from those of owls to frogs' eggs. All have a part to play in the workings of acts of witchcraft. Reason – the symbolism of the life within the shell. For the witch the same holds good for all types of nut, for they too have the outer protective shell for the germ of life within which, when released, will be productive of a new life form.'

---

98. Howard, Michael. *West Country Witches*, p.146.

Devonshire Toad Magic

Familiars & Power 🜋

We have seen in previous chapters that numerous Devonshire witches and magical practitioners were known, in one way or another, to work their magic by the aid of toads. Indeed, the West Country witch and the toad share a deep and longstanding association. A 'cunning man' who went by the wonderful name Vuzzy Jarge, lived in a village in the Blackdown Hills on the Devon-Somerset border. He was known to keep many toads in a large earthenware vessel, and would often let them out for exercise; allowing them to roam freely about his home, filling the place with a chorus of constant croaking, which visiting non-magical folk regarded as 'horrid and dismal.'

It seems that Vuzzy Jarge derived his magical powers via his relationship with his toads, including the power to curse via the use of the 'witch's circle'. He was known to hide and wait beside a path he knew his victim would soon be using. As they approached, he would jump out and mark his witch's circle in the earth around them using his walking stick. They would find themselves trapped, unable to escape from within the circle's bounds for some time, and even when they did, illness or injury would await them.[99]

Ill-Wishing 🜋

Sadly, not all practitioners viewed toads as magical allies, but purely as tools, which is when these creatures often ended up in the most unfortunate situations. The use of a toad in curse-magic appears to be illustrated within one particularly grizzly looking artefact housed within the Museum of Witchcraft and Magic. The dry remains of a toad are suspended by wire from a bizarre metal contraption of hooks and pressed brass faces. The item's

---

99. *Ibid*, p.115.

description card tells us that it was discovered hung high up in the chimney of a house in the Axminster area in 1936. This artefact has been interpreted as a curse item arising from neighbourly dislike.[100]

A Blackdown Hills 'wizard' kept toads for his own singularly unpleasant method of curse magic. When ill-wishing someone, he would select a toad, kill it, and remove the creature's heart. This would then be stuck full of pins and hung within his chimney. By doing so, the wizard hoped that as the toad heart shriveled up, so would his victim become sick and eventually die.[101]

Protective Toad Magic 🍃

Just as the toad could be used in acts of curse magic, they were also employed in Devonshire to protect from ill-wishing and the influence of the 'back witch'. Scarborough Museum's Clarke Collection includes the dried bodies two toads (which were apparently thought to be 'male frogs') contained within bags; one made of checked grey-blue fabric, the other made of very pretty fabric with a leaf design. They were hung inside cottages, the one in the blue-grey bag being hung near the cottage door, in Devonshire in the early 20th century as charms 'to keep out witches'.

Curative Toad Magic 🍃

The bodies of toads, and their parts, have an established place within the curative magic of the West Country. 'The Kings Evil' for example, and sores in any limb, were cured in Devon by the patient being given part of a toad's body, corresponding with the afflicted part of their own body, enclosed within a little bag to be worn as a charm.[102]

---

100. Museum of Witchcraft & Magic, description card for object no.138.

101. Howard, Michael. *West Country Witches*, p.115-116.

102. *Folklore Transactions in the Devonshire Association.*

Another cure charm for the King's Evil required the body of a toad to be baked until it was thoroughly dried. It would then be ground into a powder, with a stone pestle and mortar, and mixed with powdered vervain. This mixture was to then be sewn into a silken bag and worn around the neck of the patient.[103]

A Devonshire remedy for staunching blood also requires powdered toad, which was produced via a lengthy process. As speed is of course a vital necessity to the operation of blood stopping, this toad powder would be made in order to be kept for use when required.

One should gather the body of particularly large toad, three bricks, and prepare a fiercely hot fired oven. Place the bricks into the oven and keep them there until they are red hot.

When this is achieved, remove one of the bricks from the oven, and place the remains of the toad upon it; leaving it there until the brick has cooled. Repeat this process with the other bricks until the heat has reduced the body to ashes. This toad-ash powder is then to be sewn up into a silk bag, one and one half inch square. This charm bag may be kept for use when someone is bleeding, whereupon it should be placed upon the patient's heart and it will 'instantly stay the bleeding of the nose or any wound.' [104]

A similar Devonshire charm was used exclusively for nose-bleeds. The bodies of one or two 'fine old toads' were placed in a cold oven, and the heat increased until the bodies had been reduced to a 'brown crisp mass'. This was then to be removed from the oven and ground into a powder in a stone pestle and mortar. The powder was then kept in a snuff box to be snorted when required. [105]

---

103. Hewett, Sarah. *Nummits & Crummits*, p.76.

104. *Ibid*, p.81.

105. *Ibid*, p.76.

A cure for dropsy (œdema) was made by taking the bodies of several 'large fully-grown toads', and placing them in a clean vessel in which they would be heated until reduced to ashes, and in which these ashes would not become contaminated with any foreign matter. These would then be removed and placed into a stone pestle and mortar to be pounded into a fine powder, and then stored in a dry place inside a sealed wide-mouthed jar. One teaspoonful of the ashes was to be administered in milk to the patient 'at the growing of the moon' for nine mornings.[106]

As it was traditionally believed that toads were immune to the venom of adders, or 'vipers' as they were known in the West Country, a Devonshire cure charm against an adder bite was to lay the skin of a toad upon the wound in an act of sympathetic magic.[107]

Skin diseases were cured by use of 'the poison found in a toad's head'. This was extracted and enclosed within a leather bag, one inch square, and this in turn was enclosed within a white silken bag. This charm was hung upon a cord; long enough so that as the patient wore it the bag would lie upon the pit of their stomach. After the charm bag had been worn for three days, the patient would be sick. The charm was then removed and buried in the ground. As it rotted, the patient would recover.[108]

A certain amount of confusion seemed to surround the difference between toads and frogs in the West Country. What we know to be toads, were thought by some to be 'male frogs', and there was a belief that both were the same creature, but that there were two kinds; 'wet toads' and 'dry toads'. The 'wet toads', found in and around ponds, are of course frogs. These were considered to be

---

106. Hewett, Sarah. *Nummits & Crummits*, 1900, p.76-77.

107. *Folklore Transactions in the Devonshire Association.*

108. Hewett, Sarah. *Nummits & Crummits*, 1900, p.66.

'of no great repute for curative properties.' 'Dry toads', or toads proper, were however the 'right sort', and of these, toads found beneath bushes of sage were deemed to be the most potent and esteemed for their magical virtues.[109]

In all dealings however with these 'strange, loveable magical creatures' possessed of the 'fairy power to bring rich rewards', one would do well to follow Cecil Williamson's advice; *'be warned – be kind to toads.'*

---

109. *Folklore Transactions in the Devonshire Association.*

BIBLIOGRAPHY

Baring-Gould, Sabine. *A Book of the West; Being an Introduction to Devon & Cornwall.* Methuen & Co, 1899.
– *Devonshire Characters & Strange Events.* John Lane, 1908.

Bovey, Tracy. 'Weird Tales of Old Dartmoor'. *The Cauldron* No.140.

Brand, John. *Observations on Popular Antiquities.* Charles Knight & Co, 1842.

Caple, John. *Somerset.* White Lane Press, 2007.

Collingwood, W. G. *Scandinavian Britain* (1908), Llanerch, 1993.

Crossing, William. *Gems in a Granite Setting; Beauties of the Lone Land of Dartmoor.* The Western Morning News Co, 1905.

Davies, Owen. *Popular Magic – Cunning-folk in English History.* Hambledon Continuum, 2007.

Evens, Rachel. *Home Scenes: or, Tavistock and its Vicinity.* J.L. Commins, 1846.

Farquharson-Coe, A. *Devon's Witchcraft.* James Pike, 1975.

Gary, Gemma. 'The Man in Black'. *Hands of Apostasy.* Three Hands Press, 2014.

Gent, Frank. *The Trial of the Bideford Witches.* Edward Gaskell, 2002.

Hewett, Sarah. *Nummits & Crummits.* T. Burleigh, 1900.
– *The Peasant Speech of Devon, London,* E. Stock, 1892.

H.G.T. 'Pixies or Piskies'. *Notes & Queries* No.61, 1850.

Howard, Michael. *West Country Witches*. Three Hands Press, 2010.
– 'The Cunning Man'. *The Cauldron* No. 95.

King, Graham. 'Cecil Williamson & the Witchcraft Museum'. *The Cauldron* No.136.
– *The British Book of Spells & Charms*. Troy Books, 2016.

Linton, E. Lynn. *Witch Stories*. Chapman & Hall, 1861.

Lloyd Warden Page, John. *The Rivers of Devon from Source to Sea*. Seeley & Co, 1893.

Lugger, Andrew. 'Magic Moments'. *Solicitor's Journal*, 2011.

Morgan, Levannah. *A Witch's Mirror*. Capall Bann, 2013.

Norman, Mark. *Black Dog Folklore*. Troy Books, 2016.

Northcote, Lady Rosalind. 'Devonshire Folk-lore'. *Folklore* No.11, 1900.

O'Cleirigh, Jo. 'Milpreves or Adder's Beads'. *Meyn Mamvro* No.1, 1986.

Patterson, Steve. *Cecil Williamson's Book of Witchcraft*. Troy Books, 2014.

Pennick, Nigel. *Daddy Witch & Old Mother Redcap: Survivals of the Old Craft Under Victorian Christendom*. Corner-stone Press, 1985.

Rider, Catherine. *Magic & Religion in Medieval England*. Reaktion Books, 2012.

St Leger-Gordon, Ruth E. *The Witchcraft & Folklore of Dartmoor.* Hale, 1965.

Unknown. *The Life & Prophecies of Ursula Sonthiel, better known as Mother Shipton.* Dropping Well Estate Ltd.
– *The Luton Times and Advertiser*, February 27th 1869
– *The Taunton Courier & Western Advertiser*, July18th 1860
– *The Western Daily Press*, December 9th 1924

Valiente, Doreen. *The Rebirth of Witchcraft.* Hale, 1989.

Various. *Folklore Transactions in the Devonshire Association.*

Various. *The Museum of Witchcraft – A Magical History.* The Occult Art Company, 2011.

Westwood, Jennifer. *Albion – A Guide to Legendary Britain.* Paladin, 1987.

Whitlock, Ralph. *The Folklore of Devon.* Batsford, 1977.

Williamson, Cecil. 'A Conversation with Cecil Williamson'. *Talking Stick* No.7.
– 'Close Encounter with a Demon Hound'. *The Caudron* No.78.
– magical index cards archived in the Museum of Witchcraft & Magic.
– *Whatever Happened to the Old Time Witches?* (Article).

INDEX

A

Abracadabra, 192
Adder, 152, 164, 208
Ague, 167-168, 198
Ann (Toad Witch), 24-25
Anubis, 149
Armada, 36, 39
Ash, 78-79, 91, 129, 164-166, 169, 179-180
Atlantis Bookshop, 68

B

Baring-Gould, Rev. Sabine, 23-24, 28, 30-31, 144
Beads, 108, 203
Bees, 196
Bible, 24-25, 45, 118
Bideford, 48-49, 51, 53, 57-58, 60, 64, 99
Birds, 50, 159, 185, 194, 204
Bites, 164, 208
Black witch, 16, 27, 32, 77, 78-80, 83-85, 87-92, 94-95, 99,
103, 118, 122, 189-190
Blood, 12, 30-32, 56, 58, 78-79, 81, 87, 91, 108, 121-123,
129, 160-163, 165, 207
Boiling, 83
Boils, 170
Bones, 32, 96, 108, 134, 144, 153, 157, 159, 165, 184, 187,
194, 196, 202
Books (magical), 12, 18, 31, 42, 44, 83, 88, 157
Brimstone, 169
Bruises, 61, 173
Bryant, Molly, 99-100
Buckfast Abbey, 37
Buckfastleigh Church, 148, 150
Buckland Abbey, 36-37
Burn-Gout, 174
Burns, 31, 172-173

Other Books by Gemma Gary

Troy Books:

Traditional Witchcraft – A Cornish Book of Ways
The Black Toad – West Country Witchcraft & Magic
The Charmer's Psalter
The Devil's Dozen – Thirteen Craft Rites of the Old One

Three Hands Press:

Wisht Waters – Aqueous Magica and the Cult of Holy Wells

Lightning Source UK Ltd.
Milton Keynes UK
UKHW012125071020
371191UK00003B/97